FLASH POINT

Ignite Your Team and Forge a Winning Culture

Frank Viscuso

DEDICATION

This book is dedicated to you.

My hope is that the content on the following pages will help reignite your passion and provide you with the strategy and tactics needed to motivate your team members and forge a winning culture.

CONTENTS

ACKNOWLEDGMENTS

Along my personal journey in the fire service, in business, in coaching, and in life, I have met some amazing people whose names I have mentioned in the acknowledgements of many of my previous books. Every one of them have influenced me and helped shape me into who I am today. Their influence is also sprinkled throughout the pages of this book.

Thank you to my mother Mildred and my father Sebastian for providing me with the foundation.

Thank you to my brother and sister firefighters throughout the world who have encouraged me and provided me with the opportunity to share this message that I am so passionate about.

Thank you to my wife Laura and my boys Nicholas, Frankie, and Thomas for your constant and unwavering support.

INTRODUCTION

There is a certain feeling a person experiences when they are part of a winning team. It is unlike any other feeling in the world. When a group of individuals come together as a cohesive unit, take on a significant challenge, perform at an extremely high level, and accomplish an exceptional feat, they feel invincible – as if they can take on the world. Moments after an exhilarating victory, team members often feel as if nothing is impossible. After two or three victories, they become comfortable staring straight into the face of adversity, because each person understands that if anything goes wrong, those standing next to them will have their back. This is not an easy stage of team development to attain, but once you do, you will remember that team for the rest of your life, and you will strive to recapture that magic on every future team you ever become part of.

On the other hand, there are few experiences worse than being thrown into a leadership position on a struggling team that is consumed with drama and has fallen into a coma of complacency. During those times, you will find yourself spending way too much time trying to overcome your team members' bad habits, bad attitudes, and bad energy, which can be emotionally and physically draining. Unfortunately, this is all too common in today's world where many people often put the "ME" ahead of the "WE" and forget that we are here to serve "THEM."

Teams do not just randomly find themselves in the winner's bracket. There are reasons why some teams succeed, and others fail. There are endless resources that individuals like you can use to help you become a more effective leader, but these resources will not randomly fall onto your lap. You must seek them out, whether it be an online training, a team development class, a conversation with a mentor, or a book like this. Anyone on any team can learn from a winning team, regardless of the arena in which they are competing. A successful CEO of a Fortune 500 company can learn as much from the head coach of an NFL Super Bowl Championship team as the coach can from the CEO.

I have learned from many successful team leaders through their books, seminars, and one-on-one conversations. Throughout the years, I have found myself on successful teams in sports, business, and the fire service – where I worked for more than twenty-six years and served in every position, from a recruit to a tour commander and deputy chief. During my time as a firefighter, I had written seven industry-related books, including the bestsellers *Fireground Operational Guides*, *Common Valor: True Stories from America's Bravest (vol. 1)*, *Step Up Your Teamwork*, and my breakout leadership book, *Step Up and Lead*. The content provided in *Step Up and Lead* has helped so many firefighters advance their careers and personal lives that I have spent the last ten years of my life traveling throughout the world providing leadership, team development, customer service training, and keynotes for tens of thousands of people in hundreds of industries.

This book was written to provide you with the eight steps that I have relied on throughout my life to help me reach my career and personal goals as a fire service professional, author, coach, and public speaker. I am certain that these eight simple steps can also help you achieve personal success and lead your team to a better place.

I decided to write this book following an experience I had a few years after being promoted to the position of deputy chief. It happened early one morning when the alert tones came over the fire station's intercom. Many fire departments use different tones to differentiate alarms, such as investigations, EMS calls, or reports of a working fire. When the tones for a working fire come in, as they did on that day, firefighters, who always hustle, tend to move toward the apparatus a little faster, which is exactly what I did.

I hopped in my Suburban and raced to the scene. The goal was simple: arrive first, size up the situation, and provide some pre-arrival information for the other responding units. The sirens echoed through the busy streets that were still dark enough to be illuminated by spinning red lights. An engine and a ladder company, containing firefighters from my station, followed close behind. We would be the first three apparatus arriving on the scene. Another three engine companies would not be far behind. All four engine companies carried three members; the single ladder company would bring an additional four. The initial alarm would consist of seventeen total firefighters of various ranks, including myself. As the deputy chief, I would be operating as the incident commander (IC). For the sports fan, if we were a football team, the incident commander's job would be equivalent to that of a head coach. As the IC, my job is to gather as much information as I can, and call the plays, but I am not actually "on the field" physically performing the way a quarterback or wide receiver would. The IC stages at the command post and directs units as they arrive on the scene. The other firefighters on the scene execute the game plan, which in this case would include things like advancing hose lines and searching for fire and life inside the burning structure.

Engine and ladder companies have different responsibilities at a fire. For those of you reading this who are not firefighters, the specifics are not important, but to give you a general idea of what each does, an engine company's primary job is to secure a water supply and advance hose lines to protect occupants, and to locate, confine, and extinguish the fire. Ladder companies focus on forcing entry to gain access into the structure, searching for – and rescuing – trapped occupants, and ventilating the building to remove the toxic gases and smoke to make the area more survivable. There are many additional duties that members of each company perform, but that is not important for you to understand right now.

As we rushed to the scene, the dispatcher came over the radio and announced that he had received multiple calls reporting the fire, which was a surefire way of confirming that this was not a false alarm. My foot became a little heavier as I turned onto the street where the fire was. The fire building was an occupied three-story apartment complex. The smoke was heavy and had begun to form a thick haze that was lingering in the street. Ferocious flames were pushing out of various windows on the second floor. All signs indicated that this was going to be a tough fire. I informed dispatch that I was on the scene, gave an initial radio report, and called for a second alarm, which would bring two additional engine companies, one additional ladder company, and a battalion chief from a neighboring community to the scene. If we made a successful initial push, we may not need them, and I would turn them back around. If the fire turned out to be more advanced than it appeared from the outside, we would need to immediately utilize the additional personnel and resources. Calling for an upgraded assignment is a proactive measure that many seasoned fire service officers believe in because of the time it takes for units to respond from neighboring communities. Simply put, it is always better to be safe than sorry.

Traffic was halted by the police on both ends of the street as our companies began to arrive and position in front of the building that was on fire. The crew of the first arriving engine company secured a hydrant with large 5-inch supply line and connected it to the pump panel on their rig so the apparatus would have a continuous water supply. I briefly spoke with the captain of that company and gave him his assignment. He then proceeded to advance the initial attack line into the burning building to locate, confine, and extinguish the fire. The officer on the ladder company and his crew also met me at the command post for an assignment before making their way into the structure to perform their primary search for victims.

As additional companies arrived on the scene, they calmly but swiftly approached me, received their assignments, and went to work. Everyone knew their job. Everyone did their job. Everyone looked and acted as if they had been here before. At that point in my career, our team kind of reminded me of NFL Hall of Famer Barry Sanders after he scored a touchdown. Following each touchdown, Sanders, the great Detroit Lions running back, would jog over to the referee and flip him the football. There was no fancy celebration. He knew why he was on the field — to find the end zone. And when he did, he knew it was not the first time he would put points on the board, and it certainly was not going to be the last. He did not need to dance and slam the ball on the turf to make a statement. He let his ability and performance make the statement. That is what always impressed me about

Sanders, and that was the way these firefighters carried themselves – like they have been here before.

The bond that firefighters share is an exceptional one. If you have ever been part of a team where your success or failure depends greatly on the men and women who are standing to your right and left, then you understand the bond I am speaking about. It is a bond forged in the fires of adversity. It is a bond that only occurs when each individual member is willing to sacrifice everything for the success of the mission. The bond I am referring to comes from spending countless hours living and training together. An amateur wrestling team needs mat time. A basketball team needs court time. A firefighting crew needs drill time. When these teams put in the work, their competition better hope they did as well. Putting in the work, however, is only part of the equation. When two teams put in an equal amount of work, the difference between success and failure often comes down to the strength of the bond each team has developed, and how committed each member is to the person standing next to them. This team of firefighters I was working with had an exceptional bond, which is why we approached every fire or incident with confidence in our ability and a high level of commitment toward each other.

About three and a half minutes after we arrived on scene, the fire was no longer visible and the black smoke turned to white, signifying that the fire was being knocked down and was under control. It was not long after that before all occupants were accounted for and I was able to begin placing some of our companies back in service so they could return to quarters and begin preparing for the next incident. After patting a couple of our members on the back and thanking them for another job well done, a civilian onlooker approached me from behind.

"That was impressive," the voice said.

I turned to see the familiar face of an old high school classmate that I had not spoken to in many years. So many, in fact, that I could not immediately recall his name.

"Hey, buddy, how have you been?" I asked.

He shrugged his shoulders and motioned with his head and eyes toward his vehicle, which was unluckily trapped between the curb and a charged yellow 5-inch-diameter hose line that was supplying the engine with water from a nearby hydrant. It was clear that he could not move his vehicle until we disconnected the line and drained the water from the hose. He explained that he was driving down the street as we turned the corner and pulled over to let my vehicle and the fire engine pass by, assuming he would be able to back out after we passed. Unfortunately, his car was in between the hydrant and the fire, so the vehicle was immediately blocked in by our supply line. It was a simple case of being in the wrong place at the wrong time, and it happens often at fire scenes throughout the country.

"I'm sorry about that," I said once I realized what had happened. "I'll have my team break it down so you can get where you are going."

"I'm in no hurry. I was on my way to a business meeting. I wish every one of my co-workers could have witnessed what I just did. I was serious when I said that was impressive. I'd love to know your secret."

"Our secret?" I asked, unsure to what he was referring.

"Yes. There was no hesitation. No confusion. Everyone knew exactly what they were doing, and they looked great doing it. You must have fires like this every day," he replied.

It was a satisfying comment for me to hear since we were only averaging about one fire every month at the time. One of the mantras we continuously told ourselves was that every day we came to work we should expect a fire, and at every fire we should expect to have to make a rescue. On the days when we do not have fires or rescues, we will train for the days when we do. The comment my friend had just made validated that our work ethic had been paying off.

"If I could get my team to work the way yours does, it would eliminate all our problems. That type of teamwork does not just happen. It's deliberate."

After a brief conversation, I turned away and directed the engine crew to break down the supply line, and my old friend was free to go. We shook hands, and he was on his way. I looked around at the firefighters who were picking up their tools and accounting for their equipment, and then I glanced at the officers who were gathering information for their reports. I suppose I never sat back to think about it before, but my friend was right. When this group of individuals went to work, they really were quite impressive. They were a fully developed, highly effective team. They were champions in their arena, and they proved their value every day they came to work.

A few days later, I could not stop thinking about what my friend had said about our team – *"There was no hesitation. No confusion. Everyone knew exactly what they were doing, and they looked great doing it,"* and *"If I could get my team to work the way yours does, it would eliminate all our problems. That type of teamwork does not just happen. It's deliberate."*

It occurred to me that he was right. A well-trained team of firefighters move swiftly, with specific intent and definitive purpose. To the untrained eye it can sometimes resemble chaos, but fire service professionals operate in a rapidly changing environment that requires the ability to continuously adapt, execute, and overcome adversity. Firefighters inherit risk on the fireground, but this team of professionals I was lucky enough to work with trained hard, so they did not create additional, unnecessary risk through faulty actions and poor decision making. They were not perfect, and they would be the first to admit it, but they strived to be the best that they possibly could, and that was why they were able to get the job done time and time again.

People in leadership positions really can learn valuable team-building principles by watching a successful fire department operate on the fireground or at any of the life threating incidents they regularly respond to. If a CEO, business owner, coach, or parent stopped and watched competent and proficient firefighters working at a three-alarm fire, they would be impressed by how everyone knows their job, commits to their job, and aggressively tackles their assignment, while being ready to adapt when necessary. People leading teams would find great value in the concept of unit cohesiveness, and that is exactly what this book will help you achieve.

Flash Point: *Ignite your team and forge a winning culture*, will introduce you to the four stages of fire and how they relate to the four stages of team development. A person who recognizes which stages his or her team is in will have a better idea as to which behaviors their team members must avoid, and which ones they must strive to exhibit to become a high-functioning team. The primary focus of Flash Point will be the eight steps that were referenced a moment ago. Those who understand and implement these steps will have a tremendous advantage over a those who does not. The advantage I am referring to is that of a group of individuals coming together, finding their flash point, and becoming a fully developed team.

A Flash Point is the temperature at which a particular organic compound gives off sufficient vapor to ignite in air. The flash point is the lowest temperature needed for ignition.

An organic compound can be 1 degree away from its flash point, meaning it is hot,

but has not ignited. Add one additional degree, and it will result in instant ignition. The same phenomenon can happen with a team. You may be thinking your team is working hard, meeting quotas, training daily, and putting in the work, but you just aren't seeing the results you want and expect, and you cannot figure out why. You may be consistently wonder, "What are we doing wrong?"

The answer may be quite simple. You could be doing almost everything you need to be doing but missing one simple step, and that may be what is making all the difference – one degree of difference. This book will help you find that extra degree so you can help your team reach their Flash Point and forge a winning culture. This book will thoroughly cover each of the eight steps you absolutely must take to lead a team to the pinnacle of success, which we will refer to as the fully developed stage of team development.

If you are not a firefighter and you are still skeptical as to whether these principles will translate into your chosen field, rest assured that they will. I have personally applied these same principles to achieve team-oriented success in many arenas outside the fire service, including the development of two top-producing sales teams and several championship athletic teams. If applied correctly, I am confident they can help you achieve success in your chosen field as well.

The Four Stages of Team Development

In my book *Step Up Your Teamwork*, readers were introduced to the four stages of fire and their relation to the four stages of team development:

- The incipient stage
- The growth stage
- The fully developed stage
- The decay stage

These stages represent how a fire initiates, progresses to a fully developed stage, and eventually burns out. For this analogy, you will want to imagine that your team is the fire, and your goal is to become fully developed. A team will regularly move from one stage to another. No team stays in one place. They are either moving forward or falling behind – increasing or decreasing. This is mainly because teams, like people, are constantly either progressing or regressing. It is not possible to achieve success and create momentum without taking actions to sustain or improve upon your position.

Each of the four stages present their own unique challenges to a group of people who are striving to work together as a cohesive unit. As you continue reading, think about which stage best describes your current situation. This will help you to have a better understanding of what actions need to be taken to support your team's quest for success.

Here is an explanation of what each stage is in terms of fire development. This will help you understand how each can be categorized as a team development stage.

Incipient – This first stage of fire begins when heat, oxygen, and a fuel source combine and have a chemical reaction resulting in fire. This is also known as "ignition" and is usually represented by a small fire which sometimes goes out on its own, before the next stage is reached. Recognizing a fire in the incipient stage provides people with the best chance at suppression or escape.

Incipient as a team development stage: This is when a group of people initially come together with intentions of accomplishing a shared purpose and goals. The team may be small, but they have ignited and are ready to start producing. In this stage, you usually have a combination of new members and seasoned veterans. One or two dinosaurs may be on the team as well. The term "dinosaur" is not meant to reference a person's age. It is meant to reference their disposition. Dinosaurs do not like change, and therefore are usually not contributors in a positive sense. They are on the verge of extinction. When a team in the incipient stage burns out, like some incipient fires do, it's usually a result of a negative energy of dinosaurs or the inability of people in leadership positions to encourage and inspire their team members to work together.

Growth – The growth stage is where the structure's fire load and oxygen are used as fuel for the fire. There are numerous factors affecting the growth stage, including where the fire started, what combustibles are involved or nearby, room size, ceiling height, and the potential for "thermal layering." It is during this shortest of the four stages when a deadly flashover can occur.

Growth as a team development stage: In this stage, a team will begin to develop a philosophy, implement a plan, and produce results. Those results can be good or bad, but they are a sign that something is happening. Teams may also encounter challenges, such as disagreement about mission, vision, core values, or strategy. During this stage, team members are getting to know each other, and therefore strained relationships and conflict may occur. This may be the result of clashing personalities, but it can also be the handiwork of the dinosaur philosophy of "change is not good." This is an important stage because with the right energy, philosophies, and guidance, you can lead your team to the next, most important phase. It is essential to understand that conflict does not have to be a bad thing. Conflict comes from a difference of passionate viewpoints, which is a result of a person's personal life experiences. When people with opposing viewpoints have respect for each other, they can overcome their differences. We will dive deeper into that thought process and discuss conflict resolution later in this book. A team can easily move through the growth stage into the fully developed stage with a well-defined plan of action along with a sense of urgency. When there is urgency, production tends to increase. When there's lack of urgency, there's complacency, and complacency is the enemy of progress.

Fully developed – When the growth stage has reached its maximum and all combustible materials have been ignited, a fire is considered fully developed. This is the hottest phase of a fire.

Fully developed as a team development stage: This is where you want your team to be. Teams in this stage have consciously or unconsciously formed working relationships that are enabling progress on the team's objectives. Strong relationships, team processes, and the team's effectiveness in terms of working on objectives are synching to form a successfully functioning cohesive unit. When your team reaches this stage, systems are now in place, momentum is strong, team members have begun mastering skills, and the team has reached its flash point. This stage can only be achieved when a team is passionate about their purpose. You will know you have reached peak performance when the team is functioning so well that members believe it is the most successful team that they have ever been part of.

Decay – Usually the longest stage of a fire, the decay stage is characterized a significant decrease in oxygen or fuel, putting an end to the fire.

Decay as a team development stage: This is the one stage you do not want to be in. Morale is low. Energy levels have decreased, and the team seems distracted, unfocused, and consumed with drama. In this stage you will hear team members complaining about how bad things are instead of focusing on how to make things better. This is the most dangerous stage for a team to be in because everything you have worked to build is on the verge of collapse. You can come back from the decay stage, but it will take focus, hard work, and a united effort. Passion and purpose are two key factors that you will need to focus on in to get the team back in the game, and you will need a game plan, which is what this book will provide you with.

Teams do not necessarily move through these stages in order. Many times, new team members can be the catalyst that will help the team move quickly from one stage to another. This can be a good or bad thing, depending on the energy, experience, and desire these members bring to the team. A dedicated group of veterans and a focused leader will help direct the energy of all members in the right direction. The goal of all team members should be to avoid the decay stage at all costs because it is the most difficult stage to survive.

Your team may not be in the fully developed stage right now; however, if they are, you certainly want to take the correct actions to sustain that position. Perhaps they are in the incipient or growth stage, both common stages where the proper guidance and activity can move you in the right direction. Regardless of where they are, there is good news. Whichever stage your team is in, you will need to follow the same eight steps to move them from there to where you want them to be. Each chapter in this book was written to explain one of the eight steps that will help your team become fully developed. They are, in sequential order:

Step 1 – Set Expectations Up Front:
Every organization's culture is created by design or default.

Step 2 – Prepare for Victory:
Teams often win or lose long before their games begin.

Step 3 – Take Action:
Procrastination is the slayer of confidence.

Step 4 – Delegate to Develop:
Dividing tasks and developing people multiplies your chances of success.

Step 5 – Have the Guts to Persist:
At some point in a fight, technique gives way to heart and determination.

Step 6 – Adapt When Necessary:
You must have a contingency plan for adversity because you will encounter some.

Step 7 – Serve All and Serve Well:
Always strive to exceed customer expectations—not sometimes, always.

Step 8 – Reward Your Team:
The people who work the hardest are often those who feel the most appreciated.

Eliminating or poorly executing one of these steps can have a serious negative impact on the outcome you desire. On the pages that follow, you will be provided with a game plan on how you can effectively lead your team from the incipient stage to a fully developed, functioning, cohesive unit.

In the process of learning and implementing these eight steps, you will also learn how to re-ignite your own spark to help you become a more capable leader and better version of the person you are right now.

It all begins with an investment in yourself and your culture. In this instance, that investment comes in the form of reading this book, understanding these steps, and implementing them. You must invest in your culture in such a way that it becomes stronger than the internal and external forces that will try to sabotage it. Let us get started.

1

SET EXPECTATIONS UP FRONT

Every Organization's Culture is Created by Design or Default.

As an author, I do not have any specific expectations for this book. I really do not even know what I want you to get out of it. In fact, as I am writing this sentence, I have no idea what direction I want to go in. I am simply typing the words that come to my mind and hoping for the best.

If you made it past the previous paragraph and are still reading, I am certain it is because you know that what I had written is not true. Obviously, I have expectations for this book, I know what I want you to get out of it, and I know how I want to express it. The point I am illustrating with the first paragraph is that no one gets excited about following a person who has no idea where he or she is going.

My number one expectation for this book is to provide you with a blueprint that can be used to help you achieve success in your chosen field. For starters, here are two truths that must be made abundantly clear:

1. You can make a difference.

This is the most important point that needs to be made before you proceed any further. You may have had a job or belonged to a team in which you felt like your voice did not matter. Perhaps you felt as if you were too insignificant to make a difference. This is not the case, and the sooner you realize it, the better off you and your team will be because your voice absolutely does matter and so do your ideas, actions, suggestions, and the way you treat others.

2. You can set a higher standard.

As the leader of yourself and your organization, you are the one who can set the standard for the rest of your team, so set the bar high. If you lower your standards, you are giving everyone else on your team permission to do the same. Do not go down that path. Set the bar high enough to challenge yourself and your team members. If you do so, you will likely be amazed at what you will be able to achieve when you implement these steps.

Many people in leadership positions fail at their mission for one simple reason – they fail to set the right expectations. Do not make this mistake. Without expectations, you cannot establish a game plan. Failure to plan will result in failure to execute. If you are not deliberately setting the standard and expectations for your organization, you are doing what most people do, which is show up and hope for the best. Hope is not a strategy. You must do everything with specific intent. Every organization's culture is created by design or default. This cannot be stressed enough, which is why the first step to achieving success is to set expectations for yourself and your team. To do this you must first know who you are, what you want, and how to communicate that message. The best way to start your mission is with a clear vision of where you want to end up. You need to identify what it is you are trying to achieve.

> ## Failure to plan will result in failure to execute.

Identify Your Finish Line

What are we trying to accomplish?

This is a question you will need to consistently ask yourself as well as the key players on your team. It does not matter if you are leading a team in the fire service, running a corporation, or coaching a youth sports team. You must know where you want to go so you can take deliberate action steps in that direction.

In his book *The 7 Habits of Highly Effective People*, Dr. Stephen R. Covey identifies habit #2 as *Begin with the end in mind*. Habit 2 is based on imagination. It refers to a person's ability to create in his or her mind what cannot yet be see with their eyes. This means that all things are created twice. The first is a mental creation, the second is a physical creation. It all begins with visualization followed by the creation of a culture of empowerment that will enable you and your team to create the result that you desire.

Identifying the goal requires vision. Vision combined with the ability to inspire your team is an essential quality for an effective leader to have. Without it, your team members can lose their passion and focus. There are many reasons why people leave good jobs, even ones that they love. Among the more common reasons are bad management, poor compensation, lack of advancement opportunities, and lack of job security. Even if those challenges do not exist, one of the more frustrating scenarios that many people encounter in the workplace is a team that has tremendous potential, but no one to lead them. Imagine you have big dreams and a clear vision of what you want to accomplish. Now imagine you are leading a team of high achievers, but you struggle to communicate your vision and fail to set strategic goals that will help bring those dreams to fruition. In that scenario, it is entirely possible that you may end up losing some of those team members. High achievers simply do not enjoy working under mediocre leaders who cannot define or communicate the mission.

Communicate the Mission

Three things that will help you become a more effective communicator:

1. Know who you are
2. Know what you want
3. Know how to articulate it

You must know who you are, what you want, and how to articulate it. Aristotle summed up the importance of knowing who you are and what you want with two simple words: "Know thyself." When you know who you are and what you stand for, you have the advantage over everyone who does not, because when you know thyself, you can set meaningful goals with conviction and purpose.

Imagine you are a new deputy chief and the tour commander of a shift on a one-hundred-member fire department. Your newly assigned shift has the reputation of being lazy and unreliable. Reliability is an essential quality for first responders, and it should be a non-negotiable one for you as the new commander of a shift. You have a history of setting a high standard for yourself and expecting the same from the members of you team; therefore, you know who you are and what you want. The next step is for you to communicate that message with the rest of the members on your shift. You call for a meeting, stand up in front of the team, and talk to them about the importance of being reliable. Which of the two following speeches do you think communicates this message better?

1. "You all need to be more reliable and start doing your job better." - or -

2. "Reliability is an important trait for me and an essential one for everyone in our industry. For that reason, I would like us all to hold ourselves and each other to a higher standard. I am challenging you to join me in setting the goal of becoming the go-to group on this department. To do this, we will all follow the rules, policies, and standard operating procedures of this organization. We will do our reports in a timely manner, and we will take care of our fire station the way we take care of our own homes. Reliability cannot be faked. If a person cannot be counted on to take out the garbage, wash the apparatus, or complete their reports on time, they would not be considered reliable at a structure fire. So, starting today, I would like all of us to step up our game, hold each other accountable, and set a higher standard."

Which of the two examples is more specific? I am sure you would agree that example number 1 is vague and condescending and provides no specifics with regards to why the members of the shift are considered unreliable. There is also no offering of a corrective action plan. Example number 2, on the other hand, provides more detailed information on the leader's expectations and it is obvious that this person puts the "WE" ahead of the "ME." Based on the example above, the leader in example 2 is a much more effective communicator, and chances are you would rather work for that individual.

Effective communicators are those who have learned how to persuade others. If you do not like the culture surrounding your team or organization, you need to do something about it. Be the one who is willing to persuade others and make them aware that they need to change. This is an essential responsibility for people in leadership positions, because whatever you are not changing, you are choosing. Let me repeat that: Whatever you are not changing – in your personal and your professional life – you are choosing.

> Whatever you are not changing in your organization and in your life, you are choosing.

Figure out what you believe and why, because it is not enough to simply tell people what you believe. You must tell them why you believe in it. Doing so will help you communicate with passion and purpose. You may be the most intelligent person in the world, but if you cannot effectively communicate your message, you will not be able to successfully persuade others to follow your lead.

Since the emergence of social media as one of the primary ways people communicate, many people have taken several steps in the wrong direction when it comes to effective communication and persuasion. Too many people take the low road and resort to slinging insults and trying to smear the opposing point of view instead of attempting to persuade them to see things from a different perspective. Think back to the last three presidential elections. People rarely posted positive content about the candidate they were supporting. Instead, most shared negative – even scathing – content about the opposing candidate and told everyone who was voting for that individual that they were idiots. Think about the last political argument you witnessed or engaged in on social media. Did either party involved change their mind? Probably not. What usually happens is everyone leaves the discussion angrier than they were when they entered it.

Here is a tip: You will never insult anyone to the point where they decide to agree with your perspective. Consider the last time you were insulted. Even if you were wrong, chances are you became even more dogmatic in holding your position than you were before you were insulted. If your goal is to persuade people, insulting others simply does not work.

Hypocrisy is another surefire way to fail at persuading others. You cannot live your life one way while telling other people they should do the opposite. Once again, this is never more evident as it has been on social media. Consider a teacher or principal who posts comments about how much he or she dislikes children. How would you like it if your children were under the care of that principal or teacher for six hours a day? This is the way any community would feel about the people who are supposed to be providing their services. You cannot be one person in the office or on the playing field, and completely different person in the bar or the locker room and expect people to take you seriously. This simply does not work.

Do you want to know what does work? Relationships.

Leadership is all about relationships. When people feel that you sincerely care about them, you will have the ability to be a positive influence in their life. This does not mean you should not hold people accountable for their actions, or to a high standard. On the contrary. Most parents would hold their children to a high standard because they love them and want the best for them. As the father of three boys I certainly do, and as a deputy fire chief and little league baseball coach, I did the same for every one of my colleagues and players as well.

When you communicate, make sure you are communicating a message of hope. The receiver of the message must feel that you have his or her best interest at heart. In February of 2020, America encountered an invisible enemy that was introduced as the coronavirus or COVID-19. The spread of this virus concerned public officials to the point that most states closed all schools and nonessential businesses for months. People were asked to practice social distancing and stay home unless they needed medical attention or food. During this time, people used social media platforms to communicate with each other. Many were fearful and concerned about what was going to become of the situation. Many of the messages that people were sharing early on portrayed doom and gloom, which increased the level of anxiety for many Americans. During this time, one message stood out for me more than all the others. It was a message from retired navy admiral William H. McRaven. His message was simple and to the point. That message was: "The only thing more contagious than a virus is hope."

Admiral McRaven's message was reminiscent of this memorable movie line from *The Shawshank Redemption*, when wrongfully convicted prisoner Andy Dufresne said, "Hope is a good thing, maybe the best of things, and no good thing ever dies."

If that is the type of message that your team needs to hear right now, stop waiting for someone else to share it. If you have a message and the means to communicate it, do it now. You cannot allow the morale of your organization to drop to an unsustainable level. You cannot tolerate an unacceptable standard of performance. If you do, the lower standard will become the new norm and acceptable standard for your team. The culture of any organization is shaped by the worst behavior the leader is willing to tolerate.

> The culture of any organization is shaped by the worst behavior the leader is willing to tolerate.

What is Your Mission?

To help you determine the answer to this question, consider beginning each year (or season) by meeting with your team leaders for a strategy session as I have done. For example, in the fire service, a chief officer would meet with his or her frontline officers. In sports and athletics, this meeting would be with the other coaches of your team. In sales, this meeting would be with your top producers.

During those meetings, I always began by telling each one of my team members something I appreciate about them. Positive reinforcement is important; and praising others in front of their peers has a much greater effect than doing it in private or not at all.

Some examples of praise would be:

- *I like how you come to work organized and with a plan.*

- *The way you communicate with your team (or the public) is exceptional.*

- *Your enthusiasm is contagious.*

- *You handle adversity very well.*

After recognizing each person for their strong qualities – which could include things such as organizational skills, knowledge base, positive attitude, and work ethic – it is time to start discussing who we are as a team, and where we are heading. I like to briefly talk about some of the things I would like the team to accomplish in the next three to six months, then move into the culture-building portion of the strategy session. During this part, I ask three questions. The first is, "What are we doing well that we need to KEEP doing in order to achieve better results?" The second questions is, "What are we doing wrong that we need to STOP doing in order to achieve better results?" And the final question is, "What aren't we doing that we need to START doing in order to achieve better results?" After each question, I stop talking and let the team take the lead.

Three questions to help your team achieve better results are as follows:

- What are we doing well that we need to KEEP doing?

- What are we doing wrong that we need to STOP doing?

- What aren't we doing that we need to START doing?

> Positive reinforcement is important. Praising others in front of their peers has a much greater effect than doing it in private or not doing it at all.

One year I sat down with the company officers on my shift and asked those three questions. All of them thought we needed to KEEP training as much as we had been and that we needed to KEEP providing the high level of customer service that we had come to be known for. We then discussed what we needed to STOP doing; however, the meeting really took flight when we started talking about what we need to START doing.

"You know what, Chief," one of the officers said, "if we are being honest with ourselves, we train a lot, but we aren't doing it right."

"How so?" I asked.

"Right now, a good percentage of our firefighters have less than twelve months on the job. A handful of them are straight out of the academy and have not been to a structure fire yet. Most of our drivers are new and have not been first due at a structure fire yet, and even half of the officers in this room have not been first or second on the scene at a structure fire yet. With that said, we have done more training in technical rescue, hazardous materials response, EMS, and decontamination operations than we have in basic structural firefighting," he said. Then he concluded with, "We have to get back to training on the basics."

He was right in the sense that we had been training in many specialized areas such as technical rescue and decontamination operations, but it was mainly because we had scheduled that training months earlier. He was also correct in his assessment that we had a relatively inexperienced crew, which was a result of large turnover after sudden and unplanned retirements that came about due to our governor's plan for pension and benefit reform. For those reasons, I could have responded with, "Yeah, but…" However, instead of taking that road I turned to the other officers in the room and asked if they agreed with the captain's comments about getting back to basics. They all nodded in agreement.

"Okay, so let's talk about this," I said. "We already train for three hours a day, but you are all in agreement that we need to change our area of focus and I can't argue otherwise. If we intend to be successful at a structure fire, what areas do you all feel we need to be great at?"

That question has become the same question that I ask every time I speak to fire service organizations; and every time, without fail, they all come up with the same seven areas.

1. Water supply
2. Hose line selection and deployment
3. Forcible entry
4. Search and rescue

5. Positioning ladders

6. Ventilation

7. Communication

Once we all agreed that we needed to focus on those seven main areas during our training, how difficult to you think it was for me to get buy-in from the officers in the room on implementing a back-to-basics initiative? It was not difficult at all, and why should it be? After all, I was simply implementing the idea that they came up with.

One of the goals we set for ourselves at that meeting was to continuously work to become a better version of our team every time we get back together. It was a goal of constant progress, which I often referred to as the 1 percent improvement movement. Imaging what would happen if you and your team improved by 1 percent every day. After six months, you would have a difficult time remembering what it was like being the current version of yourselves.

Setting Expectations

Imagine a team of ten individuals who have ten different sets of goals and objectives. How much do you think they will accomplish as a team? Probably not much at all. This is because they do not have one individual who is unifying them and setting clear expectations. You probably did not have to use your imagination at all because most of us have had firsthand experience on a misdirected team at one time or another.

If you are leading an organization, it is essential that you take time to identify and set expectations for your team. If you are new to an organization and you do not know the reputation or work ethic of your team members, this is not a bad thing. This is an opportunity for you to express and communicate your expectations to them. I have worked with individuals who had bad reputations when it came to work ethic, but I had come to learn that some of them were high achievers who had been previously working for people who set the bar low. They were simply performing to the level of expectations that were set by their previous team leader.

Here is an example of how this can happen. A colleague and fellow deputy fire chief once told me about the time he received a poor performance evaluation of one of his rookie firefighters. The firefighter had been on the job for three months when the chief asked his captain to complete the first of two evaluations that were to be provided during the recruit's twelve-month probationary period. The chief was surprised when he received the evaluation, because it described the firefighter as lazy, stating that he was giving a subpar performance and listed the reasons why. On that list were things like: he is always the last to help around the fire house, he lacks initiative and must be told to do everything. This was unsettling for the chief because there was a list of several hundred people who wanted the job, and he was concerned that the department may have accepted and invested in a bad candidate. At the same time, the chief was confused because every time he attended a company drill, the recruit seemed to be into the job. From his perspective, the recruit was ambitious, engaged, and energetic.

The first thing the chief did was invite the captain into his room to discuss the evaluation.

"Are we talking about the same person?" the chief asked.

"Yes, sir," the captain confirmed. "Chief, I have to tell him to do everything. He shows no initiative at all. He just sits there waiting for me to tell him to move."

"Okay," the chief said. "Bring him in here so we can have a talk with him."

The chief was disappointed to say the least, but he had to put his foot down, and the only way to do that would be to start by talking with the firefighter about his poor evaluation. When the firefighter entered the room, the chief asked him to sit down and read his evaluation so he could see for himself what the issues of concern were. After the firefighter finished, the chief asked, "Do you think that evaluation is a fair representation of who you are?"

"No, sir," the firefighter replied.

"Let me ask you this, then," the chief began. "Are you the last to get up and help out when there is work to do around the station?"

"Yes," he replied.

"And are you the last one to get up and get your gear on when it's time to train?"

"Yes," the firefighter acknowledged again.

Confused by the two contradicting answers to his initial questions, the chief followed up with one simple question: "Why?"

He did not expect the answer that he was about to receive.

"Well, Chief," the firefighter began, "on my first day at work (which was only a couple months ago), the captain told me that my job was to sit down, shut up, and don't do anything until he tells me to do it. I was just doing what I thought he wanted me to do."

The chief turned to the captain for an explanation. "Did you say that,

Cap?"

"Yes, sir," the captain replied after a momentary pause, "but I didn't exactly mean it that way."

The chief turned to the firefighter and asked him to excuse himself from the meeting so he could speak privately with the officer. As it turned out, the captain did say it to the firefighter on his first day. Imagine it is your first day at work on a new job and you are informally assigned as a mentee to someone whose responsibility it was to show you the ropes. Joining the fire service is no different. The company officer is usually the one who initially takes on the role of the mentor. On this firefighter's first day, he was standing by the apparatus during morning roll call waiting for someone to tell him what to do. After that, he was standing in the kitchen while waiting for someone to tell him what to do. At one point, one firefighter was cooking, another was setting the table, and three more were sitting down looking at their cell phones. The captain walked into the kitchen, looked at the new firefighter and asked, "What are you doing?"

The firefighter responded with, "Well, sir, I'm not exactly sure what I should be doing right now."

"I'll tell you what you to do," the captain replied. "Sit down, shut up, and don't do anything until I tell you to do it." And that is exactly what the firefighter did ... for the next three months.

There are so many things wrong with that scenario. First off, it is a terrible way to welcome a new team member onto your team. The captain was disrespectful and displayed poor leadership. The rest of the firefighters did as well. Consider the fact that three months went by without anyone telling the new firefighter what his actual job was. Anything can happen on any given day in the world of an emergency response worker. This firefighter may be the one the captain would have to rely on to save his life if things went bad on the fireground, yet he was training him to show no initiative and treating him like a child.

> ## Expectations need to be set, but they need to be the right expectations.

Many times, people in leadership positions fail to properly set expectations for new team members. This lack of communication can quickly lead to a perception of incompetence on the part of the individual who was poorly advised. After that meeting, things were set straight, and the firefighter turned out to be a valuable member on that team. He was just provided with poor direction when he initially came on the job, which led to an inaccurate perception of who he was and what he was capable of. The moral of the story is that expectation need to be set, but they need to be the right expectations.

Too many people in leadership positions do not set the right tone from the start. Many of them are simply filling a position or carrying a title. Leadership begins with setting clear expectations. Clarity is the key word to take into consideration when you are communicating with your team members. We all speak, but the words we are using are not always conveying the message we intended. Here is an example: After a successful twenty-five-year career in the fire service, one of the firefighters on my team was retiring. On his last day, the other firefighters and I decided that we wanted to do something special for him, so I told the officers in our other stations that we would be having cake and coffee at our main station at 4:00 in the afternoon. That morning, I went to the local bakery to order a cake. This bakery was known for decorating beautiful cakes; however, since I was going to be making this request only hours before our get-together, I did not know if they would have enough time to complete one for the occasion.

It was about 10:00 in the morning when I parked my deputy chief's truck in front of the bakery, entered the store, and approached the teenage girl who was working behind the counter.

"I know this is short notice, but one of the men I work with is retiring today. Would it be possible to have a cake decorated for him before four o'clock?" I asked.

"We can do that," she assured. "What would you like?"

"Just something with an engine on top," I replied.

"No problem. It should be ready by two," she assured.

Now let me paint this picture for you. I pulled up in a fire service vehicle and parked in a spot that was visible to everyone who worked in the bakery. I entered the store wearing my fire department uniform, radio and badge included, and I asked for a cake with an engine on top of it. You can imagine my surprise when I arrived to pick up the cake I ordered and discovered it had Thomas the Tank Engine sitting on top.

It would be simple for me to say, "This is not what I asked for." The problem is that it was exactly what I asked for. Although I meant a fire engine, I asked for "an engine." The young girl working behind the counter at the bakery gave me her interpretation of what I'd asked for. I did not have the heart to tell her that it was not what I meant, so I purchased the cake, and we all had a good laugh back at the fire station.

George Bernard Shaw once said, "The single biggest problem in communication is the illusion that it has taken place."

When I speak with individuals who are serving in leadership roles about being crystal clear about what it is they want to accomplish, many times I see that lightbulb go off as if they just realized, "I have not done that yet."

Maybe it is because they see themselves as a positional leader, meaning they accepted the position and with the intent of keep things status quo. That is not leadership. Maybe they do not want to get uncomfortable. That is not leadership. You must be willing to step away from familiarity to try to chart a better course, and that alone can cause significant discomfort. Consider the fact that if you are not uncomfortable in your role as a leader, you are not going to reach your potential as a leader. Because leadership is all about getting uncomfortable.

> "The single biggest problem in communication is the illusion that it has taken place."
> —George Bernard Shaw

Here are some expectations worth setting:

Once people in leadership positions commit to setting expectations, the question many ask is, "Which expectations should I set?" For starters, begin by trying to imagine the perfect teammate. What type of traits and behaviors do you want to see from them? Here are some examples of minimum standards that every organization should set for each member of their team. They must:

1. Be reliable
2. Be coachable
3. Be enthusiastic
4. Be a team player
5. Show up on time
6. Show up prepared
7. Outwork the opposition
8. Be professional and respectful

Let us dive a bit deeper into some additional expectations that are worth setting.

9. Know your job

Expect everybody to know their job and do their job. For this to happen, it goes without saying that every member of your team must know what their job is. This is true in sports, corporate America, and the emergency services. A second baseman on a youth baseball team must know that when the ball is hit to the left side of the field, his job is to cover second. If the ball is hit to the right fielder with no one on base, his job is to move to the cutoff position. On the fireground, everyone on the first arriving engine company must know what their job is. As a unit, they will secure a water supply, select the appropriate size hose line and nozzle, and advance the line to locate, confine, and extinguish the fire to protect life and conserve property. Everyone on every team MUST know their individual job and recognize how it relates to the accomplishment of the overall goal.

10. Master the basics

Professional athletes are where they are because they have mastered the basics of their sport. Successful salespeople are successful because that have mastered sales skills, like overcoming objections and closing the deal. High achievers in any arena are high achievers because they have mastered the necessary skills needed to achieve success in their chosen field. When was the last time you spoke with your team members about mastering skills? To become great at anything, you must be disciplined enough to do the basics over and over until you have mastered the basics. Talent will only get you so far, great teams are great for a reason. They outwork everyone else. Take time to figure out what skills each of your team members will need to master for you to achieve the level of success you are striving for. Then sit down with your key players and set some expectations together.

11. Always do the right thing

You already know what it legal, moral, and ethical. Be unwavering in your commitment to your team and the community you serve by being the person who always does the right thing. Be honest and show a consistent and uncompromising adherence to strong moral and ethical principles and values. Hold your team to the same standard. Doing the right thing also means performing your tasks using acceptable standards, practices, and methods. Every organization has rules, policies, or standard operating procedures. Set the right example by following them. Do every task the right way, every time. That alone will set you apart from the vast majority.

12. Hold each other accountable

Strive to develop a culture of interlocking accountability. Here is how it works. First, set the tone of intolerance for any attitude or behavior that gets in the way of developing a healthy culture. Then have everyone agree to hold themselves, and each other, accountable. Whenever someone does something right, the others should acknowledge it. Whenever something goes wrong, or someone drops the ball, instead of blaming that person or judging, acknowledge the problem exists so it can be corrected. Do this without making it personal. Support each other when mistakes are made so positive change and progress can occur. Do not become the type of organization that singles out a person and uses that individual as a scapegoat. I have seen teams that relentless pick on one person. It reminds me of a bunch of bullies picking on the weak kid in the school yard. Be better than that. Put the team first. You must, because when you get right down to it, your livelihood may depend on it.

> # Set a tone of intolerance for anything that gets in the way of developing a healthy culture.

13. Do not allow complacency to set in

In the fire service we often say, complacency kills. The National Fallen Firefighters Foundation released a list of contributing factors that led to line of duty deaths, and at the top of that list was complacency. Another thing on the list, in line with complacency, was the acceptance of accidental success, which means to accept unsafe practices and/or a low standard of performance from ourselves, our team and our equipment. Complacency may not kill people in your chosen profession, but it can kill your chances at success, and potentially destroy your team.

14. Communicate openly and honestly

When asked what they would list as the top reasons why teams fail, many people immediately say, "Communication." Without question, poor or ineffective communication is a big reason for many of the challenges we have in our lives. We are always dealing with people, so failure to communicate openly and honestly will result in a failure to solve the problems that can negatively affect your team. One of the most frequently asked questions I receive comes from people who are having challenges with one of their team members. They usually go into great details with me as to why they are having issues with that individual's attitude and/or performance. first question I always ask is, "Have you shared your concerns with the person you are talking to me about?" The point is that many of the performance problems you encounter can be solved by making all parties involved aware that the problems exist. If they do not know they are doing anything wrong, they will continue doing things the way they have been. Open and honest communication is your best way to resolve many issues.

15. Learn the rules and follow them

Most organizations have two sets of rules: formal (written) and informal or traditional (unwritten). Set the standard for your team by knowing, following, and communicating both. It is important to enforce the written rules because in the absence of rules, people make their own. They are also there for a reason. Witten rules, like standard operating guidelines, are typically the best way your organization has found to do a specific task. Ignorance to the existence of these rules is not a valid defense for those who choose not to adhere to them. If you pick and choose which ones you want to follow, you are giving permission to your team to do the same thing. Unwritten rules, or what we in the fire service refer to as tradition, are less formal but should also be followed. Do not make the mistake of misinterpreting this message. Technology changes, equipment changes, staffing levels change, and philosophies change. When it is time for change, be open to it, but unless there is a need for a change in policy or tradition, follow the rules and hold others accountable to do the same.

16. Be a problem solver

The world is full of problem finders. They exist in our communities and in the workplace. There is no shortage of people who have a problem for every solution. Do not be the problem finder on your team. Be a problem solver. The message under my signature on the emails I sent my team members was: *Never walk past a problem you can solve*. The point was a simple one. If you see the problem, solve the problem. If you cannot solve it, bring it to the attention of someone who can. Set the right example and others will follow. You will know you have a strong team when you have a team of reliable problem solvers.

There are many additional expectations that you can and should set for your team. For example, an essential team member will approach each day with a great attitude and a strong effort. In many instances attitude is more valuable than skill because a skillful individual with a bad attitude will do more harm than good to any team. On the other hand, a person who approaches daily activities and challenges with the right attitude will develop and enhance their skills in the process. If you are in a position where you do the hiring for your organization, consider hiring people with great attitudes, and training them to be skillful in their intended role.

Attitude and Effort

In 2016, University of Connecticut's women's head basketball head coach Geno Auriemma was asked why every single player on his team is so enthusiastic. Coach Auriemma began by saying that recruiting enthusiastic kids is harder than it has ever been because every kid has watched professional athletes being "really cool," and many think that is how they are supposed to act.

With regard to young players acting like they are already professionals, Coach Auriemma went on to say, "You see it all the time. You see it at every AAU tournament. You see it at every high school game. So, recruiting kids who are upbeat, love life, and love the game – have this tremendous appreciation for when their teammates do something well – that's hard. That's really hard. So, on our team, me and my coaching staff put a huge premium on body language, and if your body language is bad, you will never get in the game. Ever. I don't care how good you are."

We see this all the time in today's world. An athlete throws a tantum or a C-list actor gets arrested and suddenly gets her own reality show. How can we expect impressionable young boys and girls to act the right way when society rewards so many who do not? To prevent this attitude from infecting your team, you would have to start by raising a higher standard for yourself and your team members.

Coach Auriemma would not think twice about benching an All-American if she began acting inappropriately or selfishly. In response to other coaches saying he had the luxury of being able to do this because he had three other All-Americans on his team, Coach Auriemma said, "I get that. I understand that. But I'd rather lose than watch kids play the way some kids play (Selfishly and with bad attitudes). I'd rather lose."

As a coach of more than twenty youth baseball teams throughout the years, I can say without question that the reason why some kids in youth sports behave this way can often be tracked back to the way they are being raised. Some of today's youth are allowed to get away with being selfish and putting the "ME" ahead of the "WE." Winning a game is secondary to how many innings they played and in what positions. If a kid strikes out, I'm trying to teach them that baseball is a game of failure and that they will strike out more times than not, and to shake it off and focus on the next inning in the field and the next at-bat. At the same time, their father or mother may be standing behind the backstop, reprimanding their child for not making contact with the ball or blaming the coaches because their child sat on the bench the inning before.

During his interview, Coach Auriemma went as far as to say, "When I watch game film, I'm checking to see what's going on over on the bench. If someone is asleep over there, if somebody does not care, if somebody is not engaged in the game, they will never get in the game. Ever. And they know that. They know I'm not kidding."

There are two things you should require from every member of your team – attitude and effort. If every member on your team approaches each task with the right attitude and always give their best effort, you are going to have a productive team. You must make the point that every member on your team is important and must be ready to contribute, regardless of what position they are playing or what assignment they have been given.

Lead From Wherever You Are

Every position on a team is important. You may not be the starting shortstop for your favorite MLB team, but that does not mean your job is any less important than every other player's job is. Imagine the best shortstop in the world taking the field with eight other players who, unlike the shortstop, happen to have the worst attitude in the world. How much success do you think that team is going to have? Now imagine the entire team, including those who will spend most of their time on the bench, are all full of energy, enthusiasm, and a genuine appreciation for their role. Which team would you rather be a part of?

Mary Abigail "Abby" Wambach will go down in history as one of the greatest American soccer players of all time. Wambach, a regular on the U.S. women's national team from 2003 to 2015, was a two-time Olympic gold medalist and FIFA Women's World Cup Champion. She was a high impact forward who at the time of this writing held the honor of being the highest all-time goal scorer for the national team and was second in international goals for both male and female soccer players with a total of 184 goals. Wambach, a six-time winner of the U.S. Soccer Athlete of the Year award, was the FIFA World Player of the Year in 2012, becoming the first American woman to win the award in ten years. In addition to her athletic ability, Wambach was a leader both on and off the field. In 2015, she was listed as one of *TIME*'s 100 Most Influential People in the World.

In 2011, The U.S. women's national team, led by thirty-one-year-old Abby Wambach, placed second in the finals. It was the closest they had come to winning the title since their second FIFA Women's World Cup title twelve years earlier. Four years later, Wambach decided she wanted to play in one last World Cup before retiring, and why not—she'd co-captained and led the team for the past decade. As dominant as Wambach was on the field, Father Time is the one opponent that no athlete can defeat. Facing this reality, Wambach and her coach decided together that she would not be a starter for her final World Cup. Instead, she would come off the bench. This could not have been easy for one of the most accomplished soccer players in the world to come to terms with. The leading U.S. goal scorer would be sitting on the bench while her teammates, many of whom she mentored, would take the field at the start of the game.

Wambach had a choice to make. She had to decide what kind of a teammate she was going to be. In many interviews, she later claimed that it was one of the most difficult things that she ever had to go through. She decided that she would not just sit on the bench. Instead, she would lead from the bench. She embraced her new role and provided emotional fuel for her teammates every way that she could throughout the tournament. The U.S. women's team won the World Cup that year and Wambach later said that the pride she felt about how she handled that tournament rivaled the pride she felt when scoring a big goal.

Make no mistake about it. You will feel benched at times. You'll be left off an important project, passed up for promotion, told you did not make the team, or forced to play a supporting role when you feel you have much more to offer. During these times, it's easy to get down on yourself, especially when it seems like your teammates or colleagues are getting ahead and leaving you behind, but those times present you with an opportunity to show everyone that you are a true leader.

True leaders do not only lead when things are perfect. True leaders lead all the time, period. They lead from the front lines, and they lead from the bench. You either lead everywhere, or you lead nowhere. You may not always be in the game, but you should always be mentally engaged and emotionally connected to it. You do not have to be happy about it, however, it would say a lot about who you are by the way you embrace the opportunity to encourage others and show that you are willing to lead from wherever you are placed on the team.

There is one more important point that needs to be made about leading from the bench. If you happen to be in that position and others on your team are achieving success in areas where you wish you were, it would be easy to become jealous of other people's accomplishments, especially when their success is in areas where you strive to excel. Do not get caught up in that game. When I was a young firefighter, I remember working with a senior firefighter who seemed to always be genuinely happy for other people every time he heard about someone else achieving success in other areas of their lives. I remember talking with him about this one day and commenting about how much I appreciated his disposition to which he replied, "If you cannot be happy for other people's success, you do not deserve to be successful."

I never forgot that comment and hopefully you will not, either.

> If you cannot be happy for other people's success, you do not deserve to be successful.

Ownership Mentality

Arguably one of the biggest challenges we have in America is the consistent rise of entitlement mentality. Too many people want the reward without having to work for it. We need to start reinforcing one simple principle; when a person wants something in life, they must go out and earn it, because nobody is going to show up on their doorstep and give it to them. That, in its simplest form, is ownership mentality. You must possess that type of mindset, otherwise you cannot expect the same from the other members of your organization. It does not matter if a person is brand new or if they have been with the organization for twenty-five years, ownership mentality should be required by all.

One of the members of my organization was four months away from his retirement date when he suddenly began showing signs of bitterness and frustration. This was highly uncharacteristic of him. He was one of the most knowledgeable fire service professionals I have ever known, and he loved the job. Throughout his career he embodied the characteristics you would want to have in a firefighter – courageous, knowledgeable, committed, compassionate, team player – and he represented himself and our organization the way you would want your organization to be represented. In short, he was a model firefighter; until he no longer was.

Without any obvious reasons, he began showing up to work bitter, angry, and making remarks to the other firefighters, like, "I don't care anymore," and "This place sucks." Three of the firefighters who were listening to these early morning rants had only a few months on the job, which made this even more of a concern for me. I was not initially aware of how negative the comments from this firefighter were until the third day, when I was walking past him in the morning and heard the negative comments with my own ears.

What would you do if you were in my position? You certainly cannot ignore it. Doing so would be allowing this type of behavior, which would certainly have a negative effect on the team. Firefighters put out fires. It is what they do. When you extinguish a fire, the problem goes away. As the leader of a team, you must be ready to put out small internal fires before they grow; otherwise, they can destroy your team's chemistry and momentum. This individual's attitude was a fire that needed to be extinguished.

I immediately asked my disgruntled colleague to come up to my office. As I was his deputy chief, he did not have a choice, but as I mentioned previously in the story, that this was not characteristic behavior for this individual, so I was not angry with him. I was more so concerned with what might be causing this sudden change.

He sat in the chair facing mine with an irritated expression draped over his face.

"Would you like to tell me what's going on?" I asked in a nonconfrontational tone.

Do not be too quick to judge. Be quick to listen. One of the most underutilized skills in society is that people do not listen with the intent to understand the other person. Instead, they look like they are listening; however, they are just waiting for a pause in the conversation so they can say whatever is on their mind.

After asking the question, he took a deep breath and proceeded to tell me some of the things that were bothering him. He was upset that he'd served for nearly twenty-five years but had never been promoted. He felt he was passed over by a previous chief when he should not have been. The truth was that he was not passed over; however, he believed that the chief let the list expire when he was sitting in the number 1 position even though there was a vacant officer position available for a few months before its expiration date. He then continued with a few personal reasons why he was upset. He was about to have a big change in his life with retirement staring him in the face, so I am certain that was also playing a significant role in the way he was feeling. After giving him the opportunity to share his thoughts and vent a little, I paused to make sure I absorbed everything he had just said. I was empathetic to his situation, and I wanted to try to see things through his perspective.

"I'm sorry you have been feeling the way you have," I said, "but listen, you've been an outstanding firefighter for more than twenty-four years. In fact, you're one of the best firefighters I have worked with and possibly the best ladder tower operator I know."

"Thank you, Chief," he said.

"You're welcome. The challenge I have is that we have a bunch of young, new firefighters in the other room, and we cannot afford to have you or anyone else walking around saying things like, 'I don't care anymore.'"

I could tell by the way he was listening that he knew I was right. I continued by adding, "These new guys will never know the real you. The one that I know. The one who I have learned so much from. They are only going to know the bitter, angry, upset person that walks around complaining about everything. You have a wealth of knowledge inside of you, but they are not benefiting from that. Do you remember the time you told me that when you leave the job, the most important thing for you to know is that your brothers and sisters would be taken care of?"

"Yes," he acknowledged.

"Did you mean that when you said it?" I asked.

"Yes," he confirmed.

"Great. Then I need you to help me accomplish that goal by passing your knowledge on to them, because when you walk out of that door on your last day, twenty-five years of talent, knowledge and experience are going out the door with you."

He was locked in on what I was saying.

"I need you to help me by passing on your knowledge to all of them the way you have been for the past twenty-four and half years. That is the only way that both you and I can accomplish the goal we both have, and quite honestly, you deserve to leave this job with the legacy you have earned. Don't blow it by allowing your emotions to get the better of you this late into the game."

Again, I could see he fully understood what I was talking about.

I extended my arm and reached out to shake his hand. "Can I count on you?" I asked while holding my arm steady.

"Yes, Chief, you can count on me," he replied as we sealed the agreement with a handshake.

He immediately resorted back to the firefighter I knew and respected, and he passed on as much knowledge as he could before his final day as a public servant on our department.

> **You must be ready to put out small internal fires before they grow, otherwise they can destroy your team's chemistry and momentum.**

When a team member is not performing at his or her best, you must be willing to have the hard conversation. Make it clear that everyone needs to know their job, do their job, and help others on the team. Even if you instill this mindset in people early on, you will periodically have to remind everyone of the standard you expect from them, because everybody has those moments where they say things like, "I don't care anymore." You may have those moments as well. However, be careful what you say in front of others because people are always watching and listening, and you are always influencing others. We often fail to realize this, but any time your mouth is moving, and the attention is on you, you are influencing the people around you for better or for worse. Anytime you do something simple like roll your eyes, you influence others around you. Your gestures speak, your body language speaks, and your actions speak as loud as your words. Do not fall into the trap of thinking that people know your intentions. People do not really care about your intentions. People will judge you by your actions, therefore, you should always set the right example and act the way you want them to act.

Do not just show up. Be all in. In a conversation with former Navy SEAL J. P. Dinnell on *Flashpoint: The Fire Inside Podcast*, I asked him what made his task unit commander – Jocko Willink, co-author of Extreme Ownership – different from other Task Unit Commanders. Dinnell explained that from the moment Jocko came on as their commander, he changed the tone of the unit. The first thing he did was change their name from Task Unit Bravo to Task Unit Bruiser. By renaming the team, he was providing them with a new start, which included the rethinking and revamping of the way their did things to changing the way they think. Jocko sat them down and told them that things overseas were changing, and they were going to be up against an enemy they have never seen before. One of Jockos objectives was to teach his unit to take ownership of everything that affected their ability to deploy and be successful.

Navy SEALS are often deployed to the worst areas on Earth and must engage in sustained urban combat. They cannot call timeout in a gun fight, nor can a firefighter when fighting a structure fire. For this reason, you can imagine how empowering it is to have a leader come in and establish the mindset that your team cannot blame anyone other than themselves for their failures. You can be that person for your team. Do not allow them to make excuses and point fingers. The bottom line is that people who really want something will find a way to get it. They stop looking for problems and start looking for solutions. They take ownership.

Reliability

Reliability begins in a place that we in the fire service refer to as the "soft" working environment – such as the fire station, as opposed to the "hard" working environment – the fireground. Reliability is not something that can be faked. If you are a reliable parent, you tend to be a reliable employee. If you have the tendency to miss deadlines in your personal life, you will probably do the same in your professional life. Reliability is not something that you turn on and off depending on your mood. It is a character-defining trait. Reliable people are valuable assets to any team, and they are easy to identify, as are unreliable people.

One of the simple concepts we use in the fire service to help us establish and maintain a high level of accountability is to continuously be mindful of the fact that we are problem solvers. Problem finders are everywhere. They are in our homes, our schools, our ball fields, our workplaces, our town halls, and even our churches. We have no shortage of whiners and complainers. Unfortunately, they are not endangered species. The world is full of problem finders. We need more problem solvers. That is why every job exists, including yours.

An individual who suffered a severe injury and is in pain and must be admitted to the hospital. That individual has a problem and a medical professional's job is to provide comfort and care for that patient. That is why doctors and nurses exist.

The top of a batting line-up on a high scoring baseball team presents a problem to their opponents and the opposing pitcher's job is to get his offense off the field and get his team back in the dugout so they can be the team that score the runs. Solving that problem is the job of the pitcher, as well as the other eight individuals on the field.

A couple who are moving to a new state for work have a problem and a realtor's job is to help those clients buy and/or sell their home(s) so they can move on to the next chapter of their life. They have a problem, and realtors exist to solve that problem.

A burning apartment complex presents a problem and a firefighter's job is to arrive and save lives, stabilize the incident and conserve property. That is why they exist.

Your job is to solve problems. That is why you and every member on your team exist. Before every baseball practice, I have my teams clean the dugout. Then they do it again after they are done. Why would I make them do it before if they did not make the mess? Because I want them to know what it feels like to have to clean someone else's mess. That is the best way for me to ensure they do not leave their own mess for the next team to have to clean.

This is the same mindset a fire service officer should instill in the crew he or she is leading. It starts with the simplest things. Have you ever walked into the bathroom at your workplace only to find an empty roll of toilet paper still on the roller? That is a bigger problem than it might initially appear to be. The problem is not just about the empty roll. It is also about what that empty roll says about the individual who left it there.

It says the individual is not a problem solver.

It says the individual feels that some jobs are beneath him or her.

It says the individual does not finish the things that he starts.

It says the individual does not think about anybody but himself.

It says the individual is lazy and does nothing more than the minimum requirements.

It says the individual will be the one who is nowhere to be found when you need his or her assistance.

It says the individual may find things that need attention but is likely to leave them for someone else to take care of.

Most importantly, it says that the individual is unreliable, and in most professions unreliable people are quickly outcasted, especially in the fire service. A person who proves to be unreliable in the soft environment will always be considered unreliable in the hard environment. People do not just flip a switch. Unreliability is a character trait. Unreliable individuals are a danger to themselves, their team members, and the community that they serve. They may have many years on the job, but they do not have many years of experience; because unreliable people usually repeat their first year over and over, which is why they are expendable.

> ## Unreliable individuals are a danger to themselves, their team members, and the communities that they serve.

When you visit the Massachusetts State Fire Academy, you can walk down the hallway and see custom plaques and memorabilia on the walls that were designed and made by the previous graduating recruit classes. During one of my visits, one instructor told me that during the hands-on portion of their academy training, all the recruits of the current class were provided with water bottles that they had to carry around everywhere they went. Their job was simple — do not lose the bottle. If they lost their bottle, they would have to carry a much larger water jug until they found their assigned bottle. During the classroom portion of the training, the recruits were provided with a notebook. If they lost their notebook, they had to carry around a large dry-erase board until they found it. The instructors' intent was to teach the recruits about responsibility. On the fireground, tools are essential for firefighters, and they must be able to account for them. The academy instructors are trying to instill the ownership mentality mindset into their recruits to help prepare them for success.

Are you reliable?

Can your team members count on you?

You can rest assured that the members on your team already have their opinion of you and everyone else they work with. The question you should ask yourself is, how can I show my team that I am reliable, and make them know they can count on me? The answer is in your daily actions. Do you practice what you preach? Do you walk the walk? There are plenty of parents who tell their kids to clean their room, but they do not clean their own room. At what point do you think the child will be old enough to realize this? The same can be said about your actions, or inactions at work. Set the example for others to follow.

Certain of Purpose

As a deputy fire chief my belief was that everything that happened on my shift was a direct reflection of my leadership. If the firefighters performed well, they deserved the credit; however, if they performed poorly, it is my shift, my watch, my fault. That does not mean that they were excused and not held accountable for a poor performance or bad attitude. It simply means that if I expect them to possess ownership mentality, then I must do the same.

This type of mentality begins with your belief system.

What do you believe in? Do others think your beliefs and goals are irrational? If so, that might not be a bad thing. In January of 2007, people were saying that no one wanted a seven-hundred-dollar phone without a keyboard. It was irrational thinking. Steve Jobs thought otherwise, and the iPhone was born. His belief system changed the way most of us live today. Having and sticking to your belief system is a good thing if you are following your moral compass.

You also need to be certain of your purpose. This takes time to develop, but people are attracted to leaders who remain calm in the midst of chaos. Remaining calm when engaged in battle is something that I tried to do at every structure fire and major incident, which is why I was happy to have the following experience one day at work.

The report of a structure fire came in through our dispatch center at around noon on a busy day in October. This day was not particularly busy with regards to service calls. Our members were busy because of training. We had an outside instructor conducting an investigation-based class on scene preservation. As with all in-house training, we would have two sessions. Half of our personnel would take the class while the other half would protect the town, then they would switch.

I had just completed my class and was driving back to my station when the call came in. It was ironic to receive the call for a structure fire because thirty minutes earlier we were explaining to the instructor that three of our members were in their probationary period and had not yet had their first structure fire. As I drove closer to the street where the fire was, I began to see smoke coming from that area, which was confirmation that this was in fact a working fire. I would be the first to arrive on scene, so it would be important that I provide a good initial radio report to alert the other arriving units as to what the conditions are and what actions will need to be taken.

The fire was coming from a rear second floor window of a two-family, residential, three-story, wood-frame constructed building. The home was sandwiched in between two other homes with only a narrow walkway between them. Thick black smoke was pushing hard from the structure, a telltale sign that the fire was in the growth stage and continuing to advance toward the fully developed stage. I positioned my vehicle out of the way so that the first arriving engine and ladder companies would be able to be set up in the most advantageous position possible, then quickly began to size-up the scene and gather information so I could ensure our team has the best chance of achieving our goals of life safety, incident stabilization and property conservation.

As I moved around the structure, looking at everything from the nearest hydrant to the number of mailboxes and doorbells – which is one way to determine how many families would be living in the home, I noticed there was a man nearby taking pictures on his cell phone. I did not think much of it at the time because firefighters are used to seeing this at every call they respond to.

The companies began arriving on the scene and I began assigning tasks to each of them. The fire was slightly stubborn, but our team was able to confine it and knock it down before it advanced any further than the two rooms that were involved when we initially arrived. Later that day, I was in my office when my brother Joe called to ask me about the fire. Joe was also a deputy chief on the same department, so it was not unusual for him to know about any significant call that we responded to; however, he said he learned about this one on social media when he saw the photos. I asked him where the photos were, and he said some guy who lives in that area posted pictures on Facebook and tagged our department. He then told me where to go to see them.

On the following morning, after my shift ended, I went onto Facebook to see the photos. I was looking forward to seeing the pictures and possibly using them in my post-incident analysis. One of the first photos the man posted was of me when I first arrived on the scene and was conducting my size-up. The caption he wrote under the photo read, "This man was the first to arrive. He was moving fast and certain of purpose." My immediate thought was that this man had just given me a wonderful compliment. Those words, "certain of purpose" made me feel like all the training we do provides individuals and teams with a sense of confidence that enables them to be able to make quick and correct decisions.

I could not have asked for a better compliment, but it reminded me of what my two youngest sons' wrestling coach used to say to them. He would walk around the room while the boys were practicing their moves and say, "Believe in your preparation." It was one of his school's mottos. At the time, the coach's son was a junior in high school. His senior year he won the New Jersey State title for his weight class and received a scholarship to Northwestern University. In 2019, he won the Division I Big 10 Champion, beating returning national champion in the finals. In 2020, he repeated as the Big 10 Champion beating another national champion in the semi-finals, and a future two-time national champion in the finals. He was voted the Big 10 tournaments outstanding wrestler after knocking off three higher-ranked opponents on his way to the title. He earned the top seed going into the national tournament that year; however, the tournament was canceled due to the COVID-19 breakout in March 2020, which shut down all sports in the country as well as nonessential businesses for a period of time. The young wrestler took the collegiate wrestling world by storm that year because he was certain of his purpose, and he believed in his preparation.

Does your team have a mission statement or motto? Does it convey the essence of ownership mentality? Plano Fire and Rescue in Texas has this simple, yet powerful vision statement: "Our very best starts today, together, and never ends in building the greatest life and property saving fire service in the country." This is a powerful message for such an accountable profession. The fire service is accountable to the public, especially during these very transparent times. When people see a fire engine rolling up to a structure fire, they lift their phones and begin recording. Many times, they livestream the event on social media. It does not get more transparent than that. Imagine being a heart surgeon performing surgery in the operating room, while a dozen civilians stand in the corner and live stream the surgery. You can expect that everyone who watches that video will have an opinion on your performance. If you perform exceptionally well, some may recognize that with a positive comment. If you do not perform well, make no mistake about it, your mistakes will go viral. This thought can be used to help propel you and your team to greater heights.

> **Believe in your preparation.**

Tell Them Why

I have had the distinct honor of being invited in to speak at West Point Military Academy several times, and as a history buff, every time I pass through the campus gates I am overcome with a feeling of patriotism. West Point was built in 1778 and was originally used a military fortress during the American Revolution. George Washington considered West Point to be the most strategic location in America because it was believed the British would one day attempt to come down the Hudson and separate New York from the rest of the colonies. Therefore, whoever controlled the Hudson had the advantage in winning the war. The area where West Point was built was chosen because the land jetted out, which allowed the Revolutionary soldiers to place a gigantic chain from one side of the river to the other, preventing British ships from entering the area.

The commanders and soldiers at West Point prided themselves in being ready for a possible attack, however, no one was ready for the great act of portrayal the Continental Army would encounter. In 1780, one of George Washington's most trusted colleagues, General Benedict Arnold, took command of the Fort. Arnold was a great combat leader, but many historians believed he felt he was being cheated out of a promotion and pay; therefore, two months after being assigned to his command position, he began collaborating with British Major John Andre with the intent of selling West Point to the British for the price of twenty thousand pounds sterling.

To communicate with his British co-conspirators, Arnold used a series of coded letters, that could only be read with the help of a cypher. One of his messages was intercepted before the takeover could happen. Andre was executed and Arnold fled to England, where he lived for nearly two decades. Arnold would become notorious as America's most infamous traitor. Today on the wall of the old cadet chapel, only one of the 36 plaques designed to honor America's Revolutionary War generals is illegible, as the consonants and vowels of Benedict Arnold's name have been scratched clean by generations of unforgiving cadets.

After the Revolutionary War ended, George Washington first proposed that West Point go from being a place of shame to a school for officers; one where the virtues of honor, courage, and duty would be perpetuated. West Point has since become steeped in tradition where presidents, world leaders and the army's most celebrated and sometimes controversial officers were, and continue to be, both educated and trained. Famous alumni include Douglas MacArthur, Robert E. Lee, George S. Patton, Norman Schwarzkopf, Jr., and former United States presidents Ulysses S. Grant and Dwight D. Eisenhower.

Today, just being accepted into West Point Academy is an achievement in and of itself. Each year, fifty thousand people begin the application process, twelve thousand formally fill out the application, and only twelve hundred male and female cadets are left standing after the smoke clears. There is a good reason for this intense vetting process. West Point instructors are trying to prepare America's future military commanders for the life and death stakes that often accompany military service. These future military leaders are young men and women fresh out of high school who must learn how to survive, evade, resist, fight, overcome, and escape.

How do they do this?

On the television series *America's Book of Secrets*, there is one episode dedicated to West Point Academy. In the episode, they discuss the complex selection process, secret traditions, and elite training that cadets experience at the world's most prestigious military academy. In the documentary, U.S.M.A. Class of 1988 graduate LTC Robert O. Kirkland, a professor of Military Science at USC, stated, "We spend a whole semester on a course called Combat Leadership. A soldier today does not want to be just told *what* to do, they want to be told *why* they are doing it. What is the purpose of an operation that we are going on? Based upon the West Point officer's education, they can explain (the why) to the soldier, so the soldier has a purpose in what they're doing."

It was comforting for me to discover that the U.S. Army was supporting the same concept that I had been promoting for years, which is to *tell people why*. When every member of the team understands WHY they are doing something, you will have a better chance of getting them to buy in to the purpose of the mission.

It is likely that you have heard co-workers complain about the new policy or procedure that your organization introduced. It usually sounds something like this: "Can you believe they want us to do this?" or "Why do we have to change the way we have been doing things for all these years?" This happened the year the members of one organization were issued individual bailout ropes and escape systems. These systems were comprised of a fifty-foot rope, an anchor hook, and a descent control device. The system was placed in a fire-retardant carry bag that was then fastened to the firefighter's turnout gear.

The challenge this organization initially encountered came in the form of the old adage: "There are two things that firefighters hate: 1. Change, and 2. The way things are." This one fell under both categories, because (1) They were now told that these systems, which added even more weight to their already heavy gear, were going to be attached to their bunker pants; and (2) They were sick and tired of being told, "This is what you are going to do now," without a thorough explanation as to why.

"This is ridiculous," their Battalion Chief (BC) would hear them saying. "Now they want us to wear this thing."

"Of course they do," another would add. "It doesn't affect them. They're in administration, they don't have to wear it, so why would they care?"

The complaints continued, and were partially warranted, because the members were not told why they were issued this new equipment. They were simply told that it was mandatory that they used it. Having previously been down this road with teams, the BC knew what would happen if their complaints were not addressed. The negative noise would continue to grow until it reached the point where the general sentiment would turn into, "I don't care anymore," or "I'm done trying." As bad as it is hearing these types of statements, the next phase is even worse. That phase is when the people who cared the most no longer say anything. They just show up, give their minimum effort, and go home. The biggest concern for any organization is when their most passionate people suddenly no longer care. The BC did not want this to happen, so he came to work, brought a group of firefighters from his shift together and showed them a video about the Black Sunday Bronx Fire.

Black Sunday occurred on January 23, 2005, when three firefighters on the New York City Fire Department (FDNY) were killed in two fires: one at a house fire in the East New York section of Brooklyn, and two at a tenement fire in the Morris Heights section of the Bronx, where four others were seriously injured.

The multiple alarm Bronx fire started on the third floor of a tenement on East 178th Street. The call was made at 7:59 AM on a cold morning the day after a blizzard. The previous snowfall resulted in response delays and the temperature caused the closest hydrant to freeze. Several engine and ladder companies along with members of Rescue Company 3 were operating on multiple floors, including six firefighters in the fourth-floor apartment, which had been illegally subdivided using drywall partitions.

While performing their operations, the fire traveled through hidden spaces, came up behind them, and forced the firefighters to the windows. Unable to reach the fire escape because of the renovations, they had no choice but to jump. Only two had an escape rope. Two firefighters were killed after the fall. The other four were severely injured. Three of them were now disabled and had to retire. One of the three passed away six years later from complications related to the incident.

After watching that video, it became abundantly clear to all the members of this organization why they were all lucky to have this new self-rescue device that could potentially save their lives if they encountered a similar incident in which they would have to bail out of the window of a building. Once the members had a better understanding as to why they had this equipment, the rumbling about how inconvenient these systems may be was replaced with a sense of gratitude toward their administration for looking out for their well-being.

The lesson was clear. Do not just tell your people what to do; let them know why they are doing it.

> The biggest concern for any organization is when their most passionate people suddenly no longer care.

When you strongly establish "the why," and your team understands their mission, you will find that you have now empowered them to start coming up with ideas on how to solve problems and perform their duties. When they contribute to the development of a plan, they are more likely to buy into that plan because they helped establish it, which is another way to help establish ownership mentality.

Chapter Recap
combustible tips to ignite your team

Every organization's culture is created by design or default. Be clear with your expectations and deliberate with your actions. If you are trying to establish a good reputation, consider taking this advice that has been given to many new fire recruits: When you see that your company is about to start a new task and you are not sure what to do, look around and identify the worst or least desirable assignment and do that task. If you always do what is easy, your life will be hard.

In the fire service we often use the phrase, never walk past kinks. This is a reference to a restricted hose line. Water puts out fire. Kinks in hose lines restrict water flow. Restricted water flow can prevent extinguishment. A firefighter operating the nozzle will know if the hose line does not have sufficient water pressure; however, he or she may not know why because they may be deep inside the structure at the seat of the fire. It could be caused by low hydrant pressure, pump failure, an ineffective pump operator, or kinks in the hose line. Insufficient waterflow can result in absolute failure of a firefighter's mission to reduce the loss of life and property and protect the weak. Without water, fires will continue to grow, and lives can be lost; therefore, if any firefighter sees a kinked-up hose line, they need to take ownership of it and solve the problem. The idea is simple; never walk past kinks on the fireground or in the fire house. Kinks are everyone's problem.

This same principle holds true in any organization. Always address abnormalities. If you see the problem, solve the problem. If you cannot solve it, bring it to someone who can. In other words, never walk past a problem you can solve

2

PREPARE FOR VICTORY

Teams often win or lose long before their games begin.

Most members of the Monroe Hills High School football team were out on the field when Coach Waltman arrived late for practice. This was not an uncommon occurrence. The coach often showed up fifteen to twenty minutes late, which led many of the players to feel as if their team was not one of his top priorities. Monroe Hills, which was a powerhouse program a decade ago, was in the middle of their fourth consecutive losing season with a 1–5 record. They had just lost four games in a row, one of which was against a team they had beat convincingly at the start of the season. The players had been lacking enthusiasm and energy for weeks now, so when Coach Waltman walked into the locker room and saw the team captain taking a nap and three of his top players looking as if they would rather be any place else but at practice, he was not happy, but he was not surprised either.

"Are you guys ready for practice?" he asked, already knowing the answer from their less-than-enthusiastic body language.

One of the players smirked and gave a half-hearted nod. The captain and the other two did not even bother to acknowledge the question. Coach Waltman walked over to the captain and tapped on his shoulder.

"Cap, the rest of the team is already on the field. What are you four waiting for?"

Wiping the cobwebs from his eyes, the captain replied, "They need more practice than we do, Coach. Maybe you can work with them for a while before we get out there."

Coach Waltman was not happy with this response. He knew the culture on his team was not what he wanted it to be, but this is the first time he realized how bad it was. He did not like it when players questioned his decisions or authority, so he knew he had to make a statement.

"Let's go! All four of you. You need to be out there with your team right now."

All but the captain left the locker room and headed out to the field to be with the rest of the team. The captain then began to move, but he was much slower than the others. This made the coach's blood pressure rise a bit higher than it already was.

"Did you hear what I said?" Coach Waltman angrily asked.

"I heard you, Coach. I'm going," he said without conviction in his voice and without increasing his pace.

"Can you move a little faster? Everyone else obviously can," Coach Waltman said with more than a hint of sarcasm.

The captain turned his back and began walking out of the locker room as he mumbled, "Not everyone, Coach. You're the one who just showed up. I've been here for twenty minutes."

What do you think the chances are of this team pulling it together and having a winning season? Obviously, they are not good. It is easy to read that scenario and think you would never let that happen to your team; however, this is the type of toxic working environment many are currently encountering – poor management, bad attitudes, lazy co-workers, unsatisfactory results, no accountability, a losing record, and poor work ethic. Does any of that sound familiar? If so, what are the chances of YOUR team having a winning season? Be careful what you allow, because the behavior you allow will become the unwritten behavioral standard and social norm of your team's culture.

This section will provide you with some valuable insight on how to prepare your team for success. A championship team is the product of a championship process. If you do not prepare to win before the game is played, you will not win on game day, unless you happen to get lucky. Hoping for a victory and relying on luck is not a good strategy. This is as true in the fire service as it is in athletics, business, health care, and every other profession. Individuals and teams often win or lose long before their games begin.

> A championship team is the product
> of a championship process.

Complacency Kills

Have you ever been part of a team of disengaged individuals who have fallen into a coma of complacency? You know the signs: the team clearly is not preforming the way they should be, people are not pulling their weight, nobody seems to care about the end results, situations that previously concluded with slam dunks are now ending with air balls, and the workplace is consumed with drama.

Perhaps you are experiencing some of those things right now. When this happens in the business world, companies fail. When it happens in athletics, teams lose. When it happens in the fire services, serious injuries can occur, or worse. That is why we simply cannot allow complacency to set in. It is also why many chief officers in the fire service cringe any time they heard about someone trying to justify a subpar performance by saying, "What's the big deal? The fire went out and nobody was hurt."

With a favorable outcome, it would be easy to agree and say, "You are right. The fire did go out and nobody was hurt; therefore, we do not need to talk about getting better. We are good enough." However, a smart team leader is aware that complacency can reveal itself in the form of a seemingly simple response like the one above.

What causes complacency to set in? There are numerous reasons. In the world we live in, we are expected to constantly find ways to do more with less. If your team is struggling to evolve and adapt to new techniques or circumstances, frustration may set in. If people are working longer hours and feeling underappreciated, it is only a matter of time before they experience burnout. Add an unhealthy dose of workplace politics or mistrust, and your team is descending into the decay stage.

Complacency is easy to recognize. You can see and hear it. You can even feel it. Sometimes it can be blatantly obvious, like when a person who used to be the first to step up and tackle assignments suddenly stops taking initiative and starts looking for shortcuts, or when a leader who used to be enthusiastic, transitions into a disgruntled manager. It is not unusual for a productive team of people who used to love coming to work to become a group of dissatisfied clock punchers who are content with doing the bare minimum, which results in a decrease in customer service satisfaction and an increase in complaints and absenteeism. Does any of this sound familiar? If so, your team may be in – or heading toward – the decay stage.

In the fire service we often say, *Complacency kills*. Those two words make such a powerful statement that I wish it as posted on a wall in every fire station, warehouse, manufacturing facility, service center, health care establishment, and locker room in the country.

Ineffective policies and procedures, flawed decision making, lack of preparedness or training, poor leadership, absence of responsibility or accountability, and extraordinary unpredictable circumstances are all listed among the root causes of firefighter fatalities. Complacency is the reason why many of those things occur.

Among the list of contributing factors that led to firefighter line-of-duty deaths is – you guessed it – complacency. Another factor on the list is the acceptance of accidental success and unsafe practices, which means to accept a lower standard of performance from ourselves, our team, and our equipment. This has been referred to as the normalization of deviance, which is the gradual process by which the unacceptable becomes acceptable in the absence of adverse consequences. Do not wait for a tragedy to occur before making the changes that need to be made. Do not allow complacency to become acceptable within your organization.

There has also been one other commonly referenced phrase in the fire service that some often say to justify why an organization is using an outdated or unsafe practice. That phrase is, "Because that's the way we have always done it." As bad of a mindset that is, it is not the worst thing a person can say when they know they are not doing the right activity. Consider the team that knows they are in the wrong, but have accepted the mindset of "We should not be doing it this way, but we are, because that's the way we have always done it."

Being aware of the wrong activity is one thing; however, accepting it and not taking the initiative to correct it is something else altogether. The wrong activity will always produce the wrong result. Complacency may not kill people in your chosen profession, but it can kill your business and destroy your team, so do not accept it in any way, shape, or form.

Establish Productive Daily Habits

Did you know that you can become overwhelmingly busy doing all the wrong activities?

Close your eyes and imagine that you have a *to-do list* in front of you that has seven activities on it. Each one must get done before the end of the day. Now imagine crossing one of those activities off the list because you completed that task, and then another, and another, and another, cutting the list down to three. How does that make you feel?

Relieved, accomplished, hopeful, productive? All of the above?

Checking items off your *to-do list* can be psychologically rewarding because human brains are wired to seek completion, and the satisfaction that accompanies it. The challenge most people create for themselves is that they do not make a *to-do list*. Therefore, they end up being distracted by less important activities. Sometimes, that distraction continues to where months will pass, and they cannot figure out why that are no closer to success than they were when they started. This is worse today than ever before, and for many, social media is a big part of the problem. If you have social media apps on your phone, go to the activity section and look at the average time you spend per day using that app. You may be surprised by the amount of wasted time you spent scrolling through others' pictures, and memes, and reading their rants about politics and life.

It is imperative that you stop lying to yourself. This begins by admitting that your daily habits may be what are preventing you from reaching your goals – assuming, or course, that you have goals. The first step is to take the time to identity what exactly you want to accomplish, which is what we have already outlined in step 1, Setting Expectations. Once you do that, it is time to set goals that will help you move in the direction of reaching those expectations.

When goal setting, you may have a hard time determining which goals are urgent and which ones are not. The same can be said about identifying which are important, and which are not. To help you navigate through this process, try this simple method. Draw four boxes and write *urgent* on the top left box, and *not urgent* on the top right box. On the left side of the boxes, write *important* next to the top box, and *not as important* next to the bottom box. Each of your goals will fall into one of the four following categories:

- o Urgent and Important
- o Urgent but Not as Important
- o Not Urgent but Important
- o Not Urgent and Not as Important.

	Urgent	Not Urgent
Important		
Not as Important		

Your goals that fall in the Urgent and Important box are clearly the ones that you should spend the most of your time and energy on. Those are the ones that will help you make the most progress in terms of achieving your goals.

When some people hear the word *habit*, they immediately relate it to something negative like smoking, drinking, spending too much time on social media, or doing something unproductive. The truth is, everyone has habits, you just need to be honest about which ones are good and which ones are not. There is a specific universal question that keeps many great firefighters up at night. That question is: "Am I ready?" All firefighters are aware that they can be called to work at an intense and challenging fire at any moment, but great firefighters fully understand that the difference between success and failure comes down to their everyday habits. They know that quality training, education, and health matters. The challenge occurs when we know something can be improved upon, but we do not do anything about it.

> Everyone has habits; you just need to be honest about which ones are good and which are not.

Some people complain about training because they do not want to be exposed. Some people in leadership positions simply do not know their job. At one of my leadership seminars in Albany, New York, I mentioned that I knew of an officer who hated to train. One day he served tuna fish sandwiches for lunch, so he had each firefighter open a can a tuna and then he booked it in the training log as a forcible entry drill. During a break, one of the attendees told me that when he was in the Navy, he had an officer who also hated to train. The officer made his crew watch the movie Under Siege and booked it as a ship security drill. What are the chances that those two crews will be ready to perform effectively when placed under pressure? Maybe they will get lucky and pull through okay, maybe they will not. The question becomes, why would anybody want to leave it up to chance?

What would you do if I could guarantee you that the most intense and challenging incident of your career is going to happen exactly three months from today? Would you take the initiative to prepare for it? Of course, you would. I cannot make that guarantee, but I can promise you that at some point your body will be tested and your physical limitations will be exposed.

It may be today, next week, or a year from now, but it is going to happen. Do not waste any more time. Ask yourself: "What can I do today to prepare for that moment?"

Whether you are a firefighter or not, there are definitive action steps you can take to prepare for your career defining moment. If you do not know where to start, here are some ideas that may help you develop productive daily habits:

1. Educate yourself

    - Read a book or publication that relates to your profession.

    - Listen to a podcast or interview from a professional in your chosen field.

    - Call a mentor and have a conversation about better ways you can do things.

2. Focus on your fitness

    - Exercise.

    - Eat healthy meals.

    - Get sufficient rest/sleep.

3. Work hard

    - Do not take shortcuts.

    - Never walk past a problem you can solve.

    - Set the standard for work ethic on your team.

4. Take mental breaks

    - Listen to music.

    - Call and talk to a loved one.

    - Do something that relaxes you or makes you feel hopeful.

The importance of self-education cannot be stressed enough. Imagine that you are holding a drinking glass that is filled with 50 percent dirt and 50 percent water. Would you drink it? Of course not. That glass represents your brain and the water and dirt represent the content that many people put into their brain every day. Now take that glass with a 50/50 mix of water and dirt and place it under a faucet that flows a nonstop stream of clean drinking water. In time, the clean water will completely replace the dirt. The same thing happens about your brain when you replace bad information with positive content and knowledge. This illustrates why it is so important to consume good content from credible sources and learn something new every day.

Allowing yourself to get overwhelmed by stress is obviously not a good habit, so step 4 is as important as steps 1, 2, and 3. Depression can be debilitating. You can fight anxiety and depression – in part – by exercising, eating right, getting enough sleep, surrounding yourself with the right people, reading and watching positive content, and doing things that you enjoy.

The habits you choose will be different than the habits that other people choose, and for good reason: you may be in a different field or trying to accomplish different goals. I am an author, coach, and professional speaker, so my habits revolve around helping to ensure I am successful in my chosen fields. Some of my friends are professional athletes, a couple of them compete in mixed martial arts and have spent many years as top-ranked UFC fighters. Their habits are significantly different than those of a non-combat athlete.

Frankie "the Answer" Edgar has had one of the most successful mixed martial arts careers in UFC history. Frankie spent more than ten years ranked as one of the top five fighters in the world in his weight class. For two of those years, he was the UFC 155-pound lightweight Champion and was considered one of the best pound-for-pound fighters in the world. On a typical day during one of his fight camps Frankie trained two times a day for six days, and three times a day on the seventh. His day began with a nutritious breakfast at 8:30 AM. His first session started at 9:30. It was a one- to two-hour live training session where he worked on wrestling, jiu-jitsu, and/or sparring. He then came home for lunch, and typically had some form of physical or muscle therapy before heading off to his second workout session for the day, which often included sparring with his boxing trainer and head coach, Mark Henry. His day also included two more nutritious meals, a healthy snack, and supplements. Anyone who has even seen a Frankie Edgar fight would agree that he appears to have an endless gas tank, but those of us who know him also knew that he stayed in "fight shape" all year around, mainly because of his outstanding work ethic and productive daily habits. My daily habits do not include submitting people and getting punched in the face, and hopefully yours will not either, but your habits will make or break you in terms of success.

Habits, discipline, and training are all connected. Habits require discipline. The word *discipline* in Greek means training. A big part of success is not being lazy. This starts with being disciplined enough to show up every day. Even when you do not feel 100 percent, make it a goal to show up and work through it, because the people who display that level of commitment and discipline are also the ones who get things done.

Another byproduct of productive daily habits is that you can virtually eliminate fear and doubt. The best antidote for fear and doubt is competence. It is not enough to just hope for the problem to go away. Educate and arm yourself with the confidence, knowledge, and ability to deal with and resolve challenges. With productive daily habits, you will eventually become the problem-solver that others look to for guidance when things go wrong, and that is something this world needs more of.

> ## The best antidote for fear and doubt is competence.

When leading an organization, be sure to provide your people with the time, tools, direction, and support they need to become successful. Then hold them to a high standard. Encourage and help your team members develop productive daily habits. Those habits, in turn, will produce great results.

A friend once introduced me to this great piece of writing by an unknown author. Think about each sentence and it will surely give you a greater understanding of the power of habit.

I am your constant companion.
I am your greatest helper or your heaviest burden.
I will push you onward or drag you down to failure.
I am completely at your command.
Half the things you do, you might just as well turn over to me, and I will be able to do them quickly and correctly.
I am easily managed; you must merely be firm with me.
Show me exactly how you want something done, and after a few lessons I will do it automatically.
I am the servant of all great men.
And, alas, of all failures as well.
Those who are great, I have made great.
Those who are failures, I have made failures.
I am not a machine, though I work with all the precision of a machine.

Plus, the intelligence of a man.
You may run me for profit, or run me for ruin;

it makes no difference to me.
Take me, train me, be firm with me and I will put the world at your feet.
Be easy with me, and I will destroy you.
Who am I? ... I am a HABIT!

Education and experience do not guarantee success. Neither does the right attitude and/or habits, but they do give you a significant advantage over those who just show up and hope for the best. You must approach each task of each day with specific intent. To do this, ask yourself, "Is what I am doing, or about to do, going to get me closer to my goal?" If the answer is yes, do it. If the answer is no, reconsider the action you were about to take and revise your strategy.

You Will Perform the Way You Practice

When my youngest son was seven, my wife and I started a travel baseball team for him and a few other talented young players. The goal was to provide these boys with an opportunity to play some organized, post-season baseball at higher level. As the manager and head coach, I organized our practices as efficiently as I could by breaking the training into four stations – hitting, pitching, infield, and outfield. We set up coaching lanes where each of our four coaches took the lead in one of the four stations. Together we ran good practices that enabled the boys to work repetitively on their skills in all disciplines.

After about ten practices, we entered out first tournament with the firm belief that our team was going to be the team to beat. The fact that a few of the other teams had been playing together for a year was irrelevant. We were confident that the skill level of our boys would be enough to overcome that slight advantage the other teams had. Two innings into that game, I realized that I could not have been more wrong. Our boys lost 17–7. The game was called by way of the mercy rule in four innings. It did not take long for me to realize why our team lost. We played the same exact game as the opposing team; however, they played at a different speed. They played with urgency. They played with specific intent. We just... well, we just played the way we had been practicing.

It was obvious we needed to adapt as we moved forward. We continued practicing in our four designated stations and enabling them to work on their skills – because unused skills fade quickly – however, we began ending every practice with a simulated game. The last thirty minutes of each practice were dedicated to taking all the skills we were teaching these young boys and having them utilize those skills in real time, scenario-based baseball training. As a result of adding urgency to our practices, the team began winning tournaments and outplaying their competition all over the field. By the time they were ten, they had won more than fifty games, including nine championships, qualified to play in the United States Amateur Baseball League World Series, and were one of the top ranked teams in the state of New Jersey by travel baseball rankings.

This made me reflect on how so many organizations often train in the fire service. Many officers in the fire service conduct their search drills in a way that resembles the following structure. First, they move some furniture around in one of the rooms at their fire station. Next, they put something inside or in front of their face piece to significantly reduce the quality of their vision to simulate a smoke-filled environment. Two firefighters then enter the room, one goes right, the other goes left – both following the wall, until they find the victim. Finally, they remove the victim from the room and conclude the drill. Fifteen minutes later, they are sitting in the kitchen, drinking a cup of coffee, and talking about last night's game.

There is nothing wrong with this type of drill. They are practicing the skill, and again, this is important because unused skills fade quickly. If you do not use the skill, you will lose the skill. The problem with this method of training is that although they are practicing the skill, they are not practicing for the speed of the game. Therefore, they are missing one of the most critical components of training, which is a sense of urgency.

One year, I was contemplating this very thing while planning a search and rescue drill for our team. At the time, our group had a handful of members who had less than six months on the job along with a couple of officers who were newly promoted and were just recently assigned to our group. With that in mind, the officers and I decided to take a different approach to this drill.

We started with a thirty-minute power point presentation that covered everything to do with search and rescue in accordance with our Standard Operating Guideline. In that class, I covered three types of search: traditional search, oriented search, and Vent-Enter-Search. I also talked about common hazards, tools, and hiding places for children who may be scared. Since we had some veteran members of our organization in the room, I asked them to share some of their search experiences with the rest of our – less experienced – team members. Do not ever forget that although experience is a great teacher, learning from other people's experience is often the best teacher.

After the presentation, we moved three teams of two firefighters into one of our three stations where they began their first evolution in which they entered the room, found the victim – which in this case was a manikin – and removed the victim to safety utilizing the tips and techniques we shared in the classroom session. In the past, this is where we would typically end the drill. Maybe the team would do one additional evolution, but many times, they would simply stand by and watch the next team or two conduct their search. However, instead of ending the drill, we immediately brought the firefighters to the stairs in the fire station and had them walk up and down ten times – nineteen steps up and nineteen steps down – while still on air.

Afterward, they were a little more fatigued and had used up a good portion of the air in their cylinders. This helped us create a more realistic scenario for the second evolution in which we immediately brought each of the teams to a second station and told them we were timing them for the remainder of the drill. In other words, now there was a sense of urgency. In the real world, a trapped civilian only has so much time before a room's survivability level diminishes, and firefighter's have a limited supply of air in their self-contained breathing apparatus (SCBA). Taking this into consideration, you can see how scenarios two was significantly more realistic to a real-world situation than scenario one was.

After they completed the second station, we immediately moved them to the third station. Now their air supply was significantly lower, they were more fatigued, and time management became even more of a priority. In this station, however, we added an additional challenge for them to overcome. In one room, for example, we turned up some music loud enough so that they would have a difficult time communicating with each other. In another station, we created an entanglement situation that the firefighters had to navigate their way through. The goal for us was to see how they would react to and solve this problem.

You may be wondering why we would want to add urgency and obstacles to our drills. The answer to this question is quite simple. Consider the fact that airline pilot Chesley Burnett "Sully" Sullenberger calmly landed a plane on the Hudson River after an unexpected bird strike at takeoff crippled both engines. Sully has repeatedly stated that he hadn't trained to land a plane on water; however, he did train to remain calm and keep his composure when things went wrong so he could work through challenges and function effectively when confronted with highly stressful situations. Like airline pilots, our goal was to create challenges during training so that our members would be better equipped to overcome challenges in the real world. A fire chief does not want to find out his or her team is not prepared at three o'clock in the morning, while standing in front of a burning building with people trapped. The time to figure things out is during training, and it has been my experience that once the battle begins, no one wishes they had practiced less.

On a side note, I had come to learn that the firefighters really enjoyed our drill. During a post-training conversation, I found out that they appreciated being placed in a scenario that was more lifelike than their previous ones. The officers also commented on how important it was that we began this training with a class that covered the information outlined in our standard operating guideline. It is not unusual for an organization with three or more groups to train differently than one another, which sometimes makes all three groups operate as if they worked for three different organizations. It is also not unusual for one of those groups to find themselves comprised of members who previously worked for several different groups, but ended up working together after retirements, promotions and transfers changed the landscape of the organization. That is where our team was at that point in time, so it was refreshing to be able to ensure that all our team members were on the same page and operating with the same goals and objectives in mind.

When you train, are you going through the motions or are you practicing for the speed of the game. If you do not put your team members in tough situation during training, it will be your fault if they cannot react to them in the real world. Do not confuse this message by developing an obstacle that a Navy SEAL could not get through. Be smart and be safe but understand that complacency is the enemy of success. For those on your team who would balk at the idea of improving the way you train under the misguided thought process of "Why change the way we have always done it?" or, "All we have to do is the bare minimum to keep our jobs." I would suggest that you remind them that minimum standards are often one step above inadequate.

> ## Minimum standards are often one step above inadequate.

Repetition, Repetition, Repetition

Every morning, I would begin my shift as a deputy chief by placing a call to each of our four fire stations. The main reason for this call was to check in and speak with each house captain about their planned activities for the day. It is no secret that people who approach each day with a task or checklist accomplish more than those who do not. Daily checklists have helped me achieve far more than I would have if I just did whatever felt right at any

59

given moment. Having structure is a good thing, and it was something that I wanted to help instill in my company officers, and this was one of the ways I hoped to be able to accomplish that.

Each call would normally begin when one of the firefighters assigned to that station would answer the phone. A typical conversation sounded something like this.

"Station 3, this is Firefighter Smith."

"Good morning, Firefighter Smith, this is Deputy Chief Viscuso. How are you this morning?"

"Good morning, Chief. I'm great, thanks for asking."

"That's good to hear. How is your family?"

"Everyone is great, Chief. How about yours?"

"I'm glad to hear that. My family is doing fantastic. I appreciate you asking about them. Is your captain available?"

"Yes, sir, hold on for a minute. I'll get him."

Think about that simple, quick exchange. It only took a few seconds; however, it told my team members who answered the phones at each station that I value every one of them. When the officer gets on the phone, the exchange begins in a similar fashion. Then I ask the following question: "What do you have planned for today?"

It is important that you know what your team is working on every day. This does not mean you should stand over their shoulder and micro-manage every move that make. It simply means you are in sync with one another, as well as the game plan being implemented for that day. If you are running a drill or the morning meeting, it is easy to know where everyone is going to be and what they have planned for the day; however, if each company has its own agenda, it would be wise for you, as the team leader, to know what each of them is working on.

One of the captains on my crew always answered the question in a way that made me recognize he was well-organized and in touch with what his team needed to work on. When I would ask "What do you have planned for today?" he would always respond with an answer like the one below.

"Chief, today we are going to go down to the Oval (one of our training sites at the time) and advance some two-and-a-half-inch hose lines. Then we are going to do some pump operations training for firefighters Masser and Zydek to help prepare them to go into our driver rotation. After that, I have a search drill planned for our truck company members so they can get some more reps in."

I loved that he had a plan for the day, but what really impressed me was that he understood the value of repetitions. In his previous profession, he worked as a personal trainer, so he understood that unused muscles fade quickly. When it comes to skill-based professions, such as a hands-on job like firefighting, unused skills fade quickly. If you do not use the skill, you will lose the skill. This is true in every profession.

If you do not use the skill, you will lose the skill.

The only way to fully prepare your team to perform exceptionally well is by putting forth consistent effort. Training must be continuous, with repetitive drills. Proper firefighting, as with any other skill-based profession, is built on a foundation of perishable skills. If you do not prepare for success, you are setting you team up to feel unnecessary pressure, because pressure is that uneasy feeling an individual has when he or she is unprepared.

Are you and your team capable of landing the big client, winning the big game, or putting out that three alarm fire? Maybe you can say yes to those questions, maybe no, either answer is a good one because at least you know where you stand. The problem is when you do not know if you are ready. Uncertainty breeds indecision and hesitation. Uncertainty causes reluctant behavior, and reluctancy reduces your chances of winning. Other byproducts of Reluctancy can be fear, stress, and anxiety. There is something you can do to alleviate that type of uncertainty – You can prepare to win!

You cannot just show up one day and expect to suddenly perform like a championship caliber team. That only happens when you put in enough time and sweat equity. The habits, techniques, and systems you develop in training will foreshadow the way you are going to perform and will ultimately determine the results you are going to achieve.

Football teams win on the practice field, Boxers win in the gym, Olympic athletes earn medals during the three years and 364 days leading up to their performance. Your team should be no different. Do not practice until you get it right, practice until you can no longer get it wrong. This can only be achieved through repetition. Perform the basics, over and over, and create muscle memory. Add time constraints to simulate urgency. Your team will need to be able to work under pressure. Train until you are mentally and physically exhausted. When your resistance is low, you are more apt to make mistakes. Put yourself in that state so you can do it during game time when the stakes are high. The opportunity to win will present itself, and when it does, it will be too late to go back in time to prepare.

> Training must be continuous, with repetitive drills. Proper firefighting, as with any other skill-based profession, is built on a foundation of perishable skills.

A professional major league baseball player may swing his bat 500,000 times before he masters his swing. In the movie *Rocky*, Mick – Rocky's trainer – motivated the boxer by telling him, "For a forty-five-minute fight, you have to train for forty-five thousand minutes. Perhaps you have taken those five hundred thousand swings or trained for forty-five thousand minutes before you joined your current team. If so, that is a great foundation.

When a football team needs a quarterback, they draft a quarterback. When a company has the need for updated technical equipment and support, they seek out an information technology specialist. When most organizations select new employees and team members, an individual's previous experience is a key factor. In the fire service, especially when it comes to volunteer organizations, we do not always have the luxury of choosing our team members. When a volunteer organization needs members, they usually take who they can get. In some career organizations, a civil service testing process, or some other predetermined ranking process, does most of the decision making for the hiring organization. At the very least, these systems limit their choices. Experience is rarely a major consideration because quite frankly, how could a person possibly practice being a firefighter unless they were somehow doing the work that firefighters do? For this reason, it takes a comprehensive training program to prepare firefighters with the skills needed to perform the necessary duties. If a firefighter is not completely comfortable using power tools, he or she will need to increase their exposure to them. The same can be said about any task that makes you or your team members feel uncomfortable.

What skills do your team members have to master? Are they using repetition during training to prepare? You must be prepared for any possible scenario that might occur when you show up for work. Some of those scenarios will occur often and others would fall into the low frequency category. Some scenarios you may only experience once in your career. How do you prepare or those? You train. Everyone on your team must know their equipment, their responsibilities, the capabilities of their team members, their operating procedures, and the acceptable techniques that they can use.

It is also important to acknowledge that in many industries, such as firefighting, you may be learning a craft that you will never master. Technology, staffing levels, building construction, and equipment are constantly changing; therefore, procedures will change along with them. That is yet another thought that keeps many great firefighters up at night. They know they will be confronted with an intense fire someday, and someone's life will rely on their ability to do the job. Great firefighters will constantly ask themselves, what can I do in this moment to prepare for that moment?

Be passionate enough about your goals to outwork everyone else because hard work can beat raw talent when people who have talent do not work hard. It would be foolish for a firefighter to claim he or she is a master of their craft and does not need to train any more than the average firefighter does. Yes, an individual may master one or more aspects of the job – as they should at a minimum – but mastery of their craft is something that needs to be strived for until the day a firefighter hangs up his or her bunker gear for the last time.

The unspoken component of greatness is endurance. You must be willing to train better, harder, and longer than the competition or that which is trying to defeat you. There are no shortcuts. Training will also uncover your flaws. If you have ever attended or watched one of my seminars, you have heard me talk about the benefits of implementing real time drills. The idea for real time drills as a training tool came by accident. One of my companies was observing another company during a drill that was occurring near a supermarket. I wanted to engage that crew, so I asked the officer how he thought it would take for his crew of four to raise the aerial ladder, access the roof, and cut a ventilation hole. He gave me his opinion as did the other members of that company. I received answers that ranged from a couple of minutes to fifteen minutes. A couple of minutes seemed unrealistic to me, and fifteen minutes was unacceptable. The thing that struck me the most, however, was that they had no idea how long it would take.

This presented a big problem. If firefighters inside a structure were struggling to put out a fire and needed quick ventilation to remove the heated gases and smoke from the structure, I would call for ventilation. Not knowing how long it would take to accomplish this task could cause all of us to miscalculate the task, which could ultimately result in a failed mission, potential serious injury, or death. I pondered the answers that I had received and wondered how I could best approach this problem. Then I remembered that my brother had once organized a drill where he timed firefighters as they accomplished a similar task.

Shortly after that conversation, I called my dispatcher and requested that they send in a mock alarm for a working fire at the site where the supermarket was. I told the officer of the ladder company to treat this training exercise the way he would at a real-world incident than I said, "Here's the scenario. We have a working fire that is getting ahead of us. I have an engine company that is being pushed back out of the building by the smoke and heat. We need the roof opened now. Have your crew do exactly what they would do. When you get on the roof, start the saw, and 'simulate' the cut. I'm timing you and the clock starts now."

I could tell the captain had questions, but I walked away, keeping my eyes on the stopwatch. He turned to his crew, gave them instructions, and went to work. It took slightly more than five minutes to set up the apparatus, raise the aerial, access the roof, and start the saw. Within seven minutes, they had begun simulating the cut. I told them I was adding one minute as a buffer, because it would take time to lift the roof and clear the hole. The task was completed in eight minutes. Now we knew exactly how long it would take to accomplish this goal at our current skill level. We had a benchmark and measuring point. This was the introduction of the "Real-Time Drill."

A few days after we completed the exercise, I had our other ladder company respond to the scene and do the same. The only difference was that I told them that the previous company had accomplished the task in eight minutes. Their competitive nature took over and they beat that time by thirty seconds. After that, we set the goal to have both companies reduce their time over the next thirty days. Real time drills became vital to our success as a fire department. We took that experience and expanded into other areas of responsibility, conducting real time drills on vehicle stabilization and extrication, engine company relay pumping, self-rescue techniques, and more. The theme of the drills came down to three words: Now we know.

Now we know how long it would take to breach a wall. Now we know the speed at which we could stabilize an overturned vehicle and remove the doors. Now we know how fast each individual could connect fifty feet of 5-inch hose from the engine to the hydrant and secure a water supply. The biggest benefit that comes from real life drills is getting a company to work together toward a common goal. They become a team, sometimes competing against another team for bragging rights, but knowing that we were all doing it for the benefit of our organization.

Train for success, and train often. Repetition builds character, muscle, skills, confidence, knowledge, and consistency. Repetition builds successful teams. To use the words of many fire service professionals, "Complain less and train more."

Ruthless Repetitions

Once you get the basics down through repetitive training, it is time to step up your game. Try to create the intensity you will encounter during high pressure situations. Firefighters typically do this by training at fire academies or conducting live burn training. The goal is to create scenarios with imperfect conditions, which will help your team learn how to perform well while overcoming distractions. The fire scene, as with most highly stressful environments, presents an abundance of distraction. If you intend to perform the way you practice, you must prepare to perform under normal and abnormal conditions. This is one of the main reasons why firefighters develop mask confidence obstacle courses which are full of challenges that require the trainees to utilize their knowledge and physical ability to complete. One of my favorite moments to witness is the obvious increase in confidence that can be seen in the face of a firefighter who just completed one of these courses. The same can be said for a group of firefighters who just found and rescued the mannequin and put out the fire at their local fire academy. It is the face of accomplishment and growing confidence. It is the same face you will see on nine-year-old baseball players when they make their first double play, or a sales professional who just landed a huge account. It is the face you will want to see your team members wearing as often as possible.

Find creative ways to put your team in challenging situations during training so they can prepare to perform well when they encounter challenges in the real world. Many Super Bowl bound football teams practice the week prior to the big game with overwhelming background noise to prepare for the sound of the crowd. Many professional mixed martial artists spar for four or five rounds for a three-round fight just to ensure they will be physically and mentally prepared to go the distance. Our team of firefighters bought into the philosophy that every day we come to work we should expect a fire, and at every fire, we should expect that someone will need to be rescued. So, on the days when we did not have fires, we trained for the days when we would.

There is no shortcut to the type of success you desire to achieve. If you are in a business where you will encounter an intense, aggressive adversary, you must train to meet that opponent with equal or greater intensity. The goal is to achieve a tactical advantage over the enemy, whether it be a fire, an athletic event, or a business transaction. When faced with adversity, you and your team will need to rely on your instincts, and your instincts are developed through proper training preparation.

> "Under pressure, you don't rise to the occasion, you sink to your level of training."
>
> —Attributed to a Navy SEAL

I once heard a Navy SEAL talk about the similarities between Special Forces and first responders (police officers, firefighters, EMTs). During his talk, he said that they both fight an enemy that can strike any time during the day or night. They both fight an enemy that can strike with an unknown size and intensity. They both fight an enemy that maneuvers rapidly, and they both fight an enemy that is impossible to beat without effective teamwork.

After discussing the similarities, he talked about the three reasons why SEALs are so good at their job. Those three reasons were:

1. Their selection process,
2. The tools and equipment they use, and
3. The way they train.

I cannot speak about your selection process. I do not know how you go about choosing the members of your team; however, I do hope that you do your due diligence when doing so. A high percentage of your success will be determined by the quality of the people you surround yourself with. Make sure they have the right attitude and aptitude, because one without the other will only take them so far.

Most teams already have the proper tools and equipment to get the job done properly, so this is usually not the reasons why teams fail. That said, having the proper tools and mastering those tools are two different things. Is your team properly trained? Are they prepared to use the tools and equipment they have access to? Those are the questions that need to be asked, and the answer lies in how you train.

The way you train will be the deciding factor as to whether your team succeeds or fails. How are you preparing for your day-to-day operations? Do you feel confident that they can perform at a high level? How about those situations you do not encounter often? Do you train for those incidents? Is your team prepared for high-risk, low-frequency events? Perhaps you can take a page out of the U.S. Army's playbook and implement the concept of ruthless repetition.

Imagine you could be a fly on the wall when an army colonel speaks to new company commanders at the Infantry and Armor School in Fort Benning about the importance of establishing a proper command climate and enhancing a team's ability to perform effectively when confronted with challenging situations. What do you think the colonel would say? Perhaps he or she would explain why they should harshly discipline soldiers who make mistakes in such a way that those individuals would be afraid to step outside an established action plan. Maybe the colonel would tell them that they absolutely must obey every single order they are given regardless of what their personal experience, training and instincts are telling them. Or would the colonel empower those under his or her charge to make educated decisions, take deliberate action, adapt when necessary, and train the men and women they are leading to do the same?

Former Army Colonel Thomas M. Feltey would know exactly what that colonel would say because he was the person who had given that talk multiple times. Colonel Feltey enlisted in the New Jersey Army National Guard in February 1988 and served as an infantryman in C/2-113 Infantry (Mechanized), 50th Armored Division. He graduated from Rutgers University, where he earned his distinguished military degree before being assigned with the 1st Brigade, 2nd Armored Division/4th Infantry Division at Fort Hood, Texas. Colonel Feltey's deployments included Cuba, Germany, and Afghanistan, and he served as the senior advisor to the Ministry of Peshmerga for the Office of Security Assistance-Iraq at the U.S. Consulate General Erbil (July 2015 to June 2016).

Colonel Feltey and I have been side by side on the battlefield many times, but not the battlefield you are thinking of. Before he became Colonel Feltey, he was Tom. Tom and I played recreation football together in our hometown of Kearny, New Jersey, when we were boys. We both played on the offensive line. He was a guard, and I was the center, and our battlefield was located on top of the hill on Belgrove Drive – known as Veterans Field. Tom was a great kid and he had one of the top qualities you would ever want in a teammate. He was reliable. That trait was a cornerstone in his life from back when he was Tom and is a trait he continued to value as a high-ranking officer in the army.

So much of what we have all learned about leadership have come from principles and practices that have been established by our armed forces, so I place high value on whenever I had the opportunity to sit down with someone like Colonel Feltey and discuss leadership and team development. During one of our conversations, he discussed the techniques he used to establish, prepare, and lead effective teams. Our discussion led to the mention of the late Harold Gregory "Hal" Moore, Jr., who was a United States Army lieutenant general, a recipient of the Distinguished Service Cross, and the first of his West Point class to be promoted to brigadier general, major general, and lieutenant general. The Movie *We Were Soldiers*, which was based on his combat experience in Vietnam, starts off with Moore (portrayed by actor Mel Gibson) moving his family to Ft. Benning Georgia where he takes command of the 2nd Battalion, 23rd infantry out of 2nd infantry division. It was a new battalion designated as an experimental unit for our Army. Their intent was to utilize enhanced air tactics to achieve success. The plan was to use helicopters to move infantrymen from one place to a point of advantage over the enemy.

Many years later, that same battalion would be commanded by Colonel Feltey, which inevitably led us into a discussion about Lt. General Moore's four principles for leaders' conduct in battle, which are:

Hal Moore's four principles for leaders' conduct in battle

1. Three strikes and you are not out.

2. There is always one more thing you can do to influence the situation in your favor, and after that one more thing, and after that one more thing, etc. etc.

3. When there is nothing wrong, there is nothing wrong, except that there is nothing wrong.

4. Trust your instincts.

The last of the four principles – trust your instincts – is the one I wanted to explore with Colonel Feltey. Our instincts are the product of our education, reading, personality, and experience. Since people come from different backgrounds that provided each of them with a variety of different life experiences that shaped who they have become, it's obvious that no two people will have the same level of awareness. Firefighters, police officers, athletes, sales professionals, medical doctors, coaches, and just about everyone else you can think of are like soldiers in the sense that they need to enhance their situational awareness, so they are able identify bad things before they happen. With that thought in mind, I asked Colonel Feltey to talk about how the army helps soldiers develop their instincts and this is what he shared.

"There is a methodology to it. We develop our subordinates through Ruthless Repetitions under varying conditions. That is what ultimately builds proficiency. Especially when you come into close contact with the enemy (which in a firefighter's case could be a structure fire). It is really about pattern recognition. Over time, experience allows you to see a lot of different patterns. These are complex patterns. These aren't simple patterns," Colonel

68

Feltey said.

When a firefighter walks into a room, for example, he or she will immediately recognize things like smoke, heat, the glow of an incipient fire the same way a soldier would walk into a certain area and recognize where the enemy's weapon or rifle is. These are simple patterns to recognize; however, with continuous training and experience, we can begin to recognize more complex patterns in varying conditions of terrain that will help enhance our ability to recognize bad things before they happen.

By using the term *varying conditions of terrain*, Colonel Feltey explained that the army wants soldiers to be able to recognize patterns in a wooded area, in the nighttime, in a wide-open area, in an urban area, in the summer, in the winter, when there is high visibility on a clear day or low visibility due to fog. To get soldiers to perform effectively regardless of their environment, the key is exposing them to many different conditions and providing them with the opportunity to constantly get in their repetitions during training. If training is done correctly, when the time comes that a soldier must perform, he or she will think, "*Hey wait a minute, I recognize this pattern.*"

The question you will want to ask yourself is, "*Is my team training in a way that will enable them to recognize bad things before they happen?*"

It is not unusual to hear a group of firefighters, after a multiple-alarm structure fire, defend poor performance by saying something like, "What's the big deal? We got the job done." This mindset does nothing to help a team improve. All it does is lead to complacency and the acceptance of accidental success which was referred to earlier in this chapter. It would benefit any organizational leader to adopt the "Ruthless Repetition" philosophy described above, which includes training that will enable your team members to recognize complex patterns that are likely to occur in certain circumstances. Doing so would enable your team to develop a more acute level of instincts, which will enhance their situational awareness.

Would you want you rescuing you?

That is a question that every firefighter should ask themselves. The knee-jerk reaction would be to answer, "Yes, of course." But I would challenge them to take a much deeper look into their soul before they answer. If you are a firefighter, let me ask you to do the same thing as you contemplate this question. If everyone and everything you loved was inside your house and a fire quickly spread through your home, trapping your family, would you want you and your crew to be the first arriving company on the scene? Hopefully, you can answer with a resounding "YES!" If so, great, continue doing what you are doing. If you hesitate to say yes because you know there are more capable, better-trained crews out there, it is time to step up your game. If you are not a firefighter, relate that question to your field. If you are a baseball player and your team is losing by one run. It is the bottom of the 9th with a runner on third and two outs, would you want to be the one stepping up to the plate? If so, keep doing what you are doing. If not, it is time to step up your game.

> "If the day ever comes that you have to fight for your life, the only thing that will determine the outcome is if you trained and prepared for that fight."
>
> —Tim Kennedy, Army Ranger, former mixed martial artist

Danger Diminishes with Competence

There will be times when you feel overwhelmed by a task. That is when your preparation will truly matter the most. If you prepared for this task beforehand by going to credible sources, learning everything you can about the risk that you are facing, and training properly, you – and your team – can become experts on the things that previously caused anxiety. The best antidote for fear and doubt is competence. You cannot just hope the problem will go away. You must obtain the knowledge and ability to deal with the problem. When a competent team encounters a challenge, they can relax, gather the details, process the situation, come up with a solution, and get the job done.

Chapter Recap
combustible tips to ignite your team

Individuals and teams often win or lose long before the game begins. The wise ones are never satisfied with mediocrity. They know complacency is the enemy. They also know they can – and must – get better, because individuals and teams never stay where they are. They are either improving or regressing – heading toward the fully developed stage or moving into the decay stage. Individuals and organizations with a lot of downtime are not very productive. A firefighter cannot pretend to be ready when he or she turns the corner and sees flames coming out of every window in the structure. They had either put in the time, or they did not. At that point, it is too late to go back and do the work. Their work ethic and preparation – or lack thereof – will be revealed.

The question you want to ask yourself is: How can I become better? The answer, in part, is to buckle up. Realize that it is going to be a lot of work, but anything worthwhile always requires hard work. Keep your eye on the reason why you are working so hard. Embrace the process. Embrace the struggles. Embrace the friction. Know that you are going to become a better, stronger, more capable leader in the process.

Right now, you may not know how you will respond to pressure until you are under pressure, but if you train the right way, you will have a much greater idea of what you are capable of. It is time to get started. Do not allow complacency to set it, establish productive daily habits, train for success using repetition, and create challenging scenarios to prepare your team to be able to perform with efficiency when under pressure. Condition yourself and your team to be able to perform in situations when most people would panic, and you are well on your way to becoming a fully developed team.

3

TAKE ACTION

Procrastination is the Slayer of Confidence

GO!

Chapter Recap
combustible tips to ignite your team

I was twelve pages into the first version of this chapter before I realized I was using way too many words to say what could be said using one simple two letter word: *GO*. The fact is, you will never achieve anything unless you try. There are two reasons why many people in leadership positions fail: (1) They do without ever thinking, or (2) They think without ever doing. Number 2 is the more common reason. If you followed the first two action steps in this book, you have already set expectations and prepared for victory, so the next step is to take action. (If you have not taken the steps outlined in those sections, go back and do so, otherwise you will fall into the category of doing without ever thinking.) One of the best pieces of advice I had ever received was from a successful entrepreneur who told me that the key to success is to get started and stop stopping. Confidence is a byproduct of achievement, and your team cannot achieve anything if they are standing on the sidelines, watching other teams play. You must get in the game. Too many people think they need to have everything figured out before they get started, and as a result, they miss end up missing their window of opportunity. You will learn more by doing than you ever would by thinking about doing, so stop procrastinating, stop overthinking, stop believing that you need to have all the answers, and GO!

4

DELEGATE TO DEVELOP

Dividing tasks and developing people multiplies
your chances of success.

Do not be a manager. You may have to plan, organize, direct, evaluate, and oversee, which are all things managers do, but you have the responsibility to do more than simply manage. You have the responsibility to lead. One of the biggest problems in business as well as the emergency services is that too many people are managing, and not enough people are getting their hands dirty. You many have heard the term, "many hands make for light work." From this point on, I suggest you revise that statement to "many *working* hands make for light work."

Here is an example to put things in perspective. Company Z is on the verge of going out of business if they do not find a way to improve their sales productivity, so they begin researching what the leading company in their field (Company A) has been doing differently. A management committee consisting of several senior managers is developed to evaluate the differences between the two companies and suggest ways to improve. One of the biggest differences is that Company Z has ten salespeople and ten managers, whereas Company A has eighteen salespeople and two managers. Company Z hires a consulting company to further investigate this problem and make suggestions. They confirmed that the main problem is too many managers and not enough salespeople.

Company Z vowed to correct this problem. They begin by reorganizing their management structure. They decide to keep their ten managers (mainly because those are the same people who voted on the restructure); however, they also agreed to add a director of operations and two other managers to their corporate structure to oversee the new incentive program they are going to implement. Now there are seven salespeople and thirteen managers. To make up for the extra work the seven will have to do, the managers develop a greater incentive program. Company Z has many meetings to discuss everything they are going to do to increase their profitability, but after six months, they are even further behind. By the end of the year, three of their employees leave to work for competitors.

That story is an example of what happens when you have too many "managers." Both companies had the same amount of people, but Company Z had fewer "working" hands. Too many organizations are like Company Z. You have the responsibility to make sure that yours is not one of them. Delegation is important, but there is a huge difference between delegating for the sake of delegating and delegating with the intent of developing competent team members.

> There is a huge difference between delegating for the sake of delegating and delegating with the intent of developing competent team members.

A Hard Lesson About Delegation:

The Treadmill Syndrome

When one of my boys was fourteen months old, he came down with an ear infection. Four days later, a slight rash appeared on his chest and back, and his fever reached 103 degrees Fahrenheit. Doctors thought this was either a reaction to a high pollen count or an indication that he had roseola – a mild viral illness that usually affects kids between six months and three years old. By the fifth day, his fever was still running high, and the rash continued to spread, covering the most of his body. On day six the rash spots began to merge and run together, resembling a bad sunburn. His arm and legs began to puff and swell up, and he began gagging and coughing up phlegm.

We spent the next three days in the hospital where my little boy went through a series of tests that included bloodwork, X-rays, and a spinal tap. Each day, the doctors would come into the room and tell my wife and me what they thought he had. One day it was meningitis, the next day it was Kawasaki disease. One doctor thought my son was suffering from Stevens-Johnson syndrome, a life-threatening skin condition in which cell death causes the epidermis to separate from the dermis.

During our time in the hospital, my wife and I were asked to make many difficult decisions concerning the treatment options for our son. I spent most of my time on the internet researching my son's symptoms and trying to find out what he was fighting, a practice that many doctors frown upon. Every time we were told something different, we were also advised about the treatment options for that specific disease. For Kawasaki, that treatment included the infusion of an immune protein through a vein. The information I was finding on credible websites about this disease contradicted some of the signs and symptoms my son had, so my wife and I opted not to go with that treatment. It was a hard decision, and one that I was second guessing throughout the rest of that day and night.

I am sure you can imagine the stress that we were under; if you have ever had to make a difficult decision regarding the care for a sick family member, I am certain you know the feeling. It was the most stressful day of my life.

Later that evening I received a call on my cell phone from my son's pediatrician.

"How is you son doing?" the doctor asked.

I filled him in on what was happening as well as the procedure the doctors wanted to perform on my son and why.

"I'm familiar with the procedure. Did you do it?" he asked.

"No," I reluctantly replied, still unsure if I'd made the correct choice.

"Good, because I think I know what's wrong with him," he replied. "I think your son has serum sickness."

He went on tell me that he had been up the past few nights trying to figure out what was happening to my son. That thought alone meant the world to me. This doctor was spending his family time trying to help my family. I am sure you can imagine how grateful I was, and still am to this doctor for his compassion and dedication. He explained that serum sickness is a type of delayed allergic response that usually appears four to ten days after exposure to an antibiotic like amoxicillin, which another doctor at my son's pediatrician's office prescribed to treat his ear infection one week earlier. The doctor also said this was the worst case he had seen in more than twenty-five years, which is probably the reason why everyone was having a hard time diagnosing it.

"What do we do?" I asked.

"Nothing. If I am right, based on his age and weight, the amount of amoxicillin he was prescribed, when he started and when he stopped taking it, the rash should start disappearing as soon as tomorrow."

The next morning, we woke up and immediately began to unbutton our son's hospital gown to see where we were at. His fever was gone, and his rash was significantly reduced. Only then did the doctors at the hospital confirm that our son had suffered from serum sickness, and thankfully, we'd made the correct choice to not move forward with that procedure the day before.

It took a couple of weeks for my son's body to return to normal in terms of his body temperature, skin color, eating habits, and ability to sleep through the night, but by the grace of God we finally made it.

One night around that time, my wife and I decided to rent a movie and relax. I went upstairs to change into something more comfortable, but I could not ignore the discomfort that I was feeling. I came back downstairs fully dressed. My wife was sitting on the couch scrolling through movie options while waiting for me, but she could immediately tell by the look on my face that I was about to ruin our evening plans.

"What's wrong?" she asked.

"Don't freak out," I began, "but I am going to the hospital."

A word of advice: In retrospect I can tell you that when you are talking to your spouse, it is probably not a good idea to start a sentence with the words *don't freak out.*

"What!? Why? What happened?" she said with obvious concern in her tone.

"Honey, I have been having an irregular heartbeat for a few days and something just does not seem right. To be safe, I just want to have it checked out," I replied.

What I did not tell my wife was that in addition to chest discomfort, I also had a numbness in one of my arms, which I knew from my emergency medical technician training could be a symptom of a heart attack or stroke. I did not think that was the case, but anytime we respond on a call where someone has similar symptoms, we always advise the person to seek medical treatment. It was time for me to take my own advice.

The doctor at the hospital ran a series of tests on me and after several hours came into the room to share his diagnosis.

"How do you feel?" he asked.

"A little better now," I replied.

"All the tests came back negative. Everything looks good. Your ticker seems to be working fine," he said.

"That's good news," I replied. "What do you think caused it?"

"Well, let me ask you a question. Are you under any stress?"

Am I under stress? Was he kidding? I work in one of the most stressful professions in the world, I live in the state that has the highest tax rate in the country, and my son was just gravely ill. At that time in my life, I felt as if I was running up a downward moving escalator. Yes, I am under stress. In addition to the challenges that come from my profession, I was feeling overworked and incredibly underappreciated by my supervisor.

Firefighters have a unique perspective on life. In most polls, we rank as one of the top five most stressful jobs in America. Over time, we learn how to perform while under stress, but that does not take away the challenges that come from working in a job where you see so many terrible things. On top of everything else I was dealing with, I had what could best be described as a mild case of post-traumatic stress disorder from years of seeing things I wish I had not seen. On the surface you would never know it because I did not think I was supposed to talk about it, so I did not. Instead, I did what many firefighters do and compartmentalized my emotions. Of course, I did not feel like telling the doctor all of this, so I simply tried to make light of the situation.

"Of course I am under stress, Doc,' I answered. "I live in New Jersey. Have you seen my tax bill?"

I cracked a smile, but he did not, which made me more interested in answering his next question more seriously.

"Let me rephrase the question. Do you try to do too much?"

"No. I don't," I answered.

Thankfully, my wife was there and answered more thoroughly.

"Yes, he does," she said. "He writes books, travels throughout the country teaching, works hard on projects at home, has two kids, and carries an extremely demanding workload."

Without missing a beat, the doctor said, "Mr. Viscuso, let me give you some advice. You need to learn how to delegate."

Although I did not say this out loud, my immediate thought was that delegation is a sign of weakness. I now know that this is flawed thinking; however, let me explain why I felt this way. At the age of twenty-one, I became a firefighter. Seven years after being sworn in, I reached the rank of captain. At the age of thirty-nine, I was a deputy chief (DC) working as a tour commander. With that position comes a lot of responsibility because our DCs worked as tour commanders and handled administrative duties. When I was not running calls and writing reports, I was training. When I was not training, I was in meetings. When I was not in meetings, I was writing standard operating guidelines or grant proposals. It was a heavy workload, but my feelings were, if I showed signs that I could not handle the workload, people would think I did not belong in that position.

Everyone, in every walk of life, deals with periods of stress and the occasional feeling of being overwhelmed. It seems as if few things burn out great employees faster than being overworked and underappreciated. When people find themselves taking on more and more work, especially without being made to feel appreciated for their efforts, they sometimes feel they are being taken advantage of, which leads to burnout.

I was burnt out. I was ultimately dealing with what I once heard referred to as "The treadmill syndrome." This is when employees who consistently have too much on their plate are highly stressed because they are trying to manage numerous responsibilities. For some people, this workload – and stress – follows them into the home causing them to work around the clock, throughout the day, every day, including the days when they should be off. When they are not working, they are stressing out about work, and when they encounter an unrelated challenge in life – like a sick child – it just adds to the stress until that person reached a breaking point. This is what happened to me. Yet, I still foolishly thought that delegation was a sign of weakness.

Once again, this is flawed thinking, but when we are uneducated on a subject, the thought process will always be flawed unless we take the time to become educated. I took the doctor's advice and scheduled an appointment with a cardiologist. One week later, he gave me the "all clear." While being evaluated, I wanted to educate myself on something I knew nothing about – delegation – so I did the same thing I had done when my son was sick: I began researching. This time about the advantages of effective delegation. After gathering information, I was able to compile this short list that I reference regularly to help keep me on track.

- What happens when you try to do it all yourself?
    1. You only have your own personal input.
    2. You fail to develop your team.
    3. You create unnecessary stress and burden.
    4. You develop health issues.

- The Advantages of effective delegation:
    1. People see you as a stronger leader, and one who has confidence in his/her team.
    2. Increases morale throughout the organization.
    3. Produces greater overall efficiency.
    4. Enables you to accomplish more.

There is a solution to the treadmill syndrome, and that is to make sure work is evenly divided and properly prioritized. Additionally, there is another tremendous advantage that comes from effective delegation, which is to create leaders who can function in your absence. This all begins with recognizing who you already have on your team, and what knowledge, talent, skills, and abilities each one of them brings to the table.

Talent, Skill, and Ability

Take a moment to contemplate those words – talent, skill, and ability. Everybody has them. What are yours? What are you good at? Do you feel your talent, skills and abilities are being utilized correctly? If you work for someone else, there is a strong possibility that you would answer NO to that question, because many people in leadership positions have not taken the time to get to know what the people around them are good at.

Now, flip the script. Are you leading a team? If so, are you guilty of making that same mistake? If you answered yes, it is time to take corrective action. It is common for people in influential positions to fall into the trap of thinking they need to be the most knowledgeable and competent person in the room; however, it would benefit you to think about it a different way. Consider the following thought: If you have more talent, skill, and ability than everyone on your team, you may have a weak team.

> If you have more talent, skill, and ability than everyone on your team, you may have a weak team.

Basketball icon Michael Jordan will undoubtedly go down in history as one of the greatest athletes who ever played the game. Jordan played fifteen seasons in the NBA, winning six championships with the Chicago Bulls. Jordan initially joined the Bulls in 1984 as the third overall draft pick. He quickly emerged as a league superstar with his ability to leap, dunk, play defense, and perform under pressure. Jordan seemed to have the ability to score from almost anywhere on the court, including slam dunks from the free throw line, which in large part earned him the nickname "Air Jordan." Although they had not won a championship in his first five years with the Bulls, Jordan had a great relationship with his coach, who had built the team around his talent. In 1989, the Bulls hired Phil Jackson as their new head coach. One of Jackson's primary objectives was to develop the other players around Jordan so the team would have more than just one weapon on the court. At first, this concerned Jordan, who thought it might make the team struggle; however, under Jackson's leadership, the Bulls won six championships in ten seasons.

It would be easy to say that winning a championship with Michael Jordan on your team is an easy task for any coach; however, consider the fact that Jackson won another five NBA championships as the coach of the Los Angeles Lakers. Jackson's eleven NBA titles as a coach surpassed the previous record of nine set by Red Auerbach. Phil Jackson understood the value that each of this team members brought to the table. He knew how to utilize their talent, skill, and ability to strengthen the team.

Take a page out of Phil Jackson's book and strive to develop a team of people who have unique strengths. After losing one playoff series because they lacked a strong defensive rebounder, Jackson brought in Dennis Rodman to fulfill that role. Rodman was great at what he did, and he did not care about putting points on the board. He understood his role was to get rebounds and pass the ball to his teammates so they can score. As a result, Rodman's contributions helped lead the Bulls to an NBA title that year.

Everyone around you is unique and has a distinct skill set. You just need to take time to get to know the areas in which each of them excels. On one of my first days as a tour commander with my newly assigned team, I brought them all together and asked one simple question: "What talent or skills do you have that can help us achieve success as a team?"

As we went around the room, I found out some valuable information about each member on my crew. One was a licensed electrician – this would be helpful when we respond to electrical emergencies. One was a contractor – who could be better to conduct drills on building construction in our community? One spoke multiple languages – a valuable skill in a community where a growing portion of the residents only spoke Spanish or Portuguese. I had called on all three of those individuals shortly after that meeting to help us mitigate incidents based on their personal skill sets.

One of the best strategies for developing a successful team is to put your aces in their places. Meaning: put the correct people in the correct positions, and then get out of their way. This is how many organizations become great. They utilized the strengths of their people. Imagine coaching a high school football team and taking the kid with the best arm, strong leadership skills, and the ability to read the defense and call audible plays… and making him your place kicker. It does not make any sense to do that, yet that is what many organizations are guilty of doing.

Put your aces in their places.

Many people who have been placed in leadership positions within their organizations make the mistake of putting the wrong people in the wrong positions. These individuals may have had an abundance of talent all around them, but they did not utilize the strengths of their team members properly. It is essential that you begin by identifying the talent, skills, and ability of each member of your team.

Once you learn the value that each team member brings to the table, make a simple chart to identify their strengths. This may be a chart that only you will see, but it can help you strategize. On the top of the column, list all the talents, skills, and abilities you want and need on your team. Down the left side, put the names of your team members. As you learn about them, place a check next to the categories they excel in. The chart categories may resemble the ones shown below:

Sample Talent, Skill, and Abilities chart: Business Teams

	Effective Communicator	Problem Solver	Adapts Easily	Interpersonal Skills	Well Organized	Educated
Team member 1						
Team member 2						

Sample Talent, Skill, and Abilities chart: Fire Department

	Teachable	Hard Worker	Good with Tools	Physically Fit	Adapts Easily	Determined
Team member 1						
Team member 2						

Sample Talent, Skill, and Abilities chart: Youth Baseball Team

	Footwork	Catching	Hitting	Fielding	Throwing	Game IQ
Team member 1						
Team member 2						

Customize the list any way you want. You can use categories like "effective communicator," "problem solver," "adapts easily," "strong interpersonal skills," "well organized," "educated," "shows initiative," "great attitude," "strong fundamentals," "teachable," and "committed to self-improvement." If you are in a trade business or the fire service, the list of skills will be different. The same can be said if you are leading a sales team or coaching an athletic team. The categories will change, but the goal remains the same. That goal is to help you identify the strengths of each of your team members so you can put your aces in their places.

Placing a checkmark or number in the box of one of your team members is great, but this does not mean that you do not need to focus on developing all your people. It simply means that you have a good understanding of who, and what, you have on your team to work with. A razorblade is sharp but cannot cut down a tree. An axe is strong but cannot cut hair. Both serve a purpose and should be used for their intended purpose. The same can be said about people and their individual skill sets.

> "Everybody is a genius, but if you judge a fish on its ability to climb a tree, it will live its whole life believing that it's stupid." —Albert Einstein

The importance of knowing the strengths of those around you cannot be stressed enough. The Tampa Bay Buccaneers entered the 2020 season with their new quarterback, six-time Super Bowl Champion Tom Brady. By the end of that season, Tom Brady was a seven-time Super Bowl Champion. Brady received a lot of the credit for improving the culture of that team and rightfully so. He helped them go from a talented group of individuals who had a difficult time winning big games, to Super Bowl 55 Champions. To give Tom Brady all the credit, however, would be overlooking the time, energy, and efforts of the other players and coaching staff. Head coach Bruce Arians, for example, had put together a diverse coaching staff, including a female assistant defensive line coach and a female assistant strength-and-conditioning coach. When asked about the diversity of his staff, and why he chose who he did, he simply replied, "Great input from different people creates great output."

Chargers, Coasters, Complainers and Corner Mutts

Firefighters begin their careers in the academy, where they receive both academic and hands-on training. The first thing recruit candidates receive is a book containing more than 1,400 pages of basic skills that every firefighter should know. Recruits are expected to learn about fire behavior, personal protective equipment, general skills, extinguishment methods, rescue techniques, tool use and care, and the best safety practices. After they receive this foundational knowledge, the hands-on live fire training begins. During that portion of the academy, recruits will participate in several training evolutions that range from search and rescue to fire suppression. The intent is to build their knowledge base and enhance their awareness as to how and why firefighters perform the tactics the way they do, as well as to help them improve their physical stamina.

When I served as my department's training officer, I liked to visit the academy on days when they conducted live fire training evolutions to see how our new recruits were doing. It was a great opportunity to watch them in action, and to get a report from the instructors who had been spending quality time with them. During my visits, I would always find time to meet with the lead instructor (LI) for a general assessment of each of our recruits. I vividly remember sitting with the LI one day at lunch as he looked across the cafeteria at our eight new recruits and quickly assessed them.

"The four on the left are **hard chargers**, those three are **coasters**, but that one is a **complainer**," he said.

No further descriptions were necessary. I knew exactly where he was coming from. In the fire service, much like in law enforcement or the military, being called a hard charger is a tremendous compliment. The opposite can be said about the other two titles. Here is a breakdown of all three:

Hard Chargers are the people who get things done. If it is true that 10 percent of the people within any organization do 90 percent of the work to make that organization run effectively, then those 10 percenters would be considered the hard chargers. They are the backbone of your team. They are the ones you can rely on do the difficult jobs because they like to work, and they take pride in completing projects and contributing to the overall mission. Chargers bring fresh ideas to the table. They get excited when you put them on the field during a championship game, and even more excited when you put the ball in their hands when the game is on the line.

Coasters are as advertised. They do their job, but not much more. There is a job description attached to their paycheck and they fulfill the minimum standard requirements that are necessary for them to receive their compensation. They rarely cause problems, but they also rarely solve them. They are not your superstars, but the good news is that many coasters are easy to influence. The bad news is if the chargers do not get to them first, the complainers certainly will.

Complainers are a problem. Complainers have a problem for every solution. That's why they are a problem. They are the people who, even when provided with ideal working conditions, tend to dwell on the negative. They always seem to find a way to sabotage a good relationship or a thriving team environment. They have an ability to suck the life out of a room and they enjoy converting other people to their way of thinking. Complainers (also known as recliner snipers) are toxic, and if you have more of them than you do chargers and coasters, your team is on life support. The only thing that can bring you back is a deliberate cultural shift.

> Complainers tend to dwell on the negative, even when they are provided with ideal working conditions.

Prior to the release of this book, which you are currently reading, artist Paul Combs and I created a children's book titled *Sprinkles the Fire Dog* (Fire Engineering, 2021). In the book, we use a new term that can be used to describe a fourth type of person, the corner mutts.

Corner Mutts are like complainers. They also have a problem for every solution, but they are often less competent than the others. This is mainly because they don't love, or care about their job and see no reason why they should do anything to become better at it. The biggest challenge with the corner mutts; however, is they love to cut others down and dimmish their worth, and they do so without ever leaving the confines of their own corners. They are equivalent of human lawnmowers. They cut everything down but never leave their own yard. They talk a good game, but in the end, they have little to no ambition, and they do everything in their power to prevent others from improving themselves and their organization.

While reading the descriptions above, it is inevitable that you mentally placed certain members of your team members into each of those four categories. My question to you is, which category do you fall into? Wait, stop…. I want you to really think about this for a moment. I am sure I know where you would place yourself, but where do you think others would place you? We all judge those around us by their actions, but for some reason we expect others to judge us by our intentions. Forget about intentions for a moment and focus solely on your actions. Do they align with those of a hard charger?

Do you lead by example? Are you the person who never walks past a problem you can solve? Do others look to you for guidance when they are confronted with work-related challenges? Are you so enthusiastic about the job that it rubs off on those around you? Do you encourage your team members to step up and lead? Is your team better because you are on it? Will you leave your organization better than you found it? If you can answer yes to those questions, then others may very well consider you to be a hard charger.

If you intend to effectively lead a team, it would be to your benefit to embrace your hard chargers. If you cultivate the right relationship with them, they will become the driving force of change. They can sometimes be brazen or direct, but with the right direction, they can also help you influence some of the individuals who fall into the coasters category and create a strong team-oriented culture. Chargers will be your go-to team members when you need to get things done.

The complainers and corner mutts need to be dealt with immediately because you cannot allow their negativity to infect the rest of your team. They are toxic and can suck the life out of you team if you do not take action to correct this behavior, which requires courage.

In *Step Up and Lead* I wrote about three types of courage that will serve you well when leading an organization. They are:

1. Moral courage – which means doing the right thing, even when it is not the popular thing.

2. Physical courage – which is the ability to function effectively and get the job done when there is physical danger present.

3. Courageous communication – which is the willingness to have the hard conversations that are often necessary to lead during challenging times.

Do not shy away from having a difficult conversation. It is easy to ignore problems and hope they go away, but they rarely do. Be the leader who always and immediately addresses issues that can have a negative effect on the team.

All four – Chargers, Coasters, Complainers, and corner mutts – may have the capability of influencing the rest of your team members. Every organization has culture creators. They are the ones who have an ability to influence and persuade those around them. The challenge for any organization is when your influencers are frustrated or disgruntled and start persuading your team with the wrong message.

It is easy to fall into the faulty mindset that you would be better off surrounding yourself with yes-men. This is not advisable. You would be better off if you had one frustrated, hard-charging culture creator in your inner circle than ten yes-men. Yes-men (yes-women included) tell you what you want to hear. They will make you feel smarter than you are because they are either afraid of your response to their opposing point of view, or they are too insecure in their own abilities to speak up.

Frustrated culture creators are often misunderstood. More times than not, they are the people who care the most. They are change agents who have been beaten down to a point where they walk around the workplace mumbling things like, "I just don't care anymore." Hopefully you see yourself as a change agent. If so, it is your job and responsibility to speak up and remind these team members that they must shake off that negativity and begin to care again. They are the most valuable assets you have on your team because they put their heart into everything they do. you can give people the tools, training, environment, and support they need to succeed, but you cannot give them the heart. It would be in your best interest to support and provide guidance for the ones who care the most. Be the support system they need. you can do this by pointing them in the right direction, helping them come up with a game plan, and then getting out of their way so they can do what they are built to do... exceed expectations.

> "If everyone is thinking alike, then no one is thinking." —Benjamin Franklin

Your goal should be to surround yourself with those who are committed to developing a team that can achieve the highest level of success possible. Therefore, surround yourself with critical thinkers who are not afraid to tell you when they disagree with you. Surround yourself with people who have the courage to choose the right way over the easy way. Surround yourself with people who are talented and put the "WE" ahead of the "ME." Do not surround yourself with yes-men, because if two of you agree on everything, one of you is not necessary.

Lions and Sheep

One year, I was conducting a series of *Step Up and Lead* workshops for firefighters working at the US naval base in Naples, Italy. Their department was made up of a combination of US and Italian citizens. During the first workshop, I could not help but to notice that for most of the morning session, a young lieutenant was talking to two of his colleagues who were sitting to the right and left of him. I found this to be quite distracting, not to mention rude. I chose not to bring attention to it during the class because the lieutenant was speaking quietly and sitting near the back. I felt my best option would be to wait until the first break and discuss it with the Chief.

During the break, I approached the chief to talk about this situation with him.

"One of your officers does not seem to be paying attention. He is talking a lot during the presentation. You may want to have a word with him," I said.

"Actually, he is paying attention." The chief explained, "Before the class he offered to sit next to two of our members who do not speak good English so he can interpret what you are saying."

I went from being slightly agitated to begin impressed. A few minutes later, that same lieutenant approached me and, in broken English, thanked me for coming to Naples. He then opened his backpack, pulled out five of my books, and asked if I would sign them.

By the condition of the pages, I could tell these books had been opened and each page turned.

"Did you read these?" I asked.

"Yes," he replied. "When they announced that you were coming here, I purchased and read your books so I could be prepared for what you would be teaching us."

I went from being impressed to being amazed. In less than three months he had read five books, and all because he wanted to be familiar with the content a speaker was going to be teaching at a four-hour workshop.

After signing the books, I approached the chief again and told him what had just occurred. I then commented about how in ten years of teaching, no one has ever purchased and read all my books just because they heard I was coming in to speak to their organization. Most people had either already read one or two, or they ordered them after I left.

"You just validated my decision," the chief replied.

"What decision?" I asked.

The chief explained that since the department had initially been formed, promotions had always been based on seniority, meaning the firefighter with the most seniority on the job would be the next to be promoted to the first-level officer position, which in this case was lieutenant. The young officer we were talking about; however, was fourth in seniority when the chief decided to break tradition and promote the person who he felt was the best option for the position.

That night, the chief and I were having dinner when we began speaking about this lieutenant again. He told me that when brought this firefighter into his office to inform him that he was going to be promoted based on his attitude, effort, and dedication, the young man became emotional and could not thank the chief enough for believing in him.

The chief went on to say, "Some organizations are full of sheep who think they are lions. Within those organizations you will often come across a lion who everyone thought was a sheep. This young man falls into that category."

Individuals leading teams must be aware of who they have on their team. It would benefit leaders to see themselves as casting agents who are responsible for choosing the right people to fill important positions within their organization. After you identify your star players, and put them in the right position, let them grow and become the leaders (or lions) they were meant to be.

> Some organizations are full of sheep who think they are lions. Within those organizations you will often come across a lion who everyone thought was a sheep.

Manage Outcomes, Not Processes

"The morale in my organization is terrible," a director fire chief once told his chief of administration.

The administrative chief asked why he felt that way, and he elaborated by saying that he had recently sent out a notice to all the members of his organization asking for volunteers to join a newly forming public relations committee. The goal of the committee would be to plan and organize an annual open house event where the members could socialize and connect with the citizens of the community they serve. The notice had been sent out three weeks earlier, but no one responded.

"How could they possibly expect to have the support of this community when they put absolutely no effort into developing a relationship with them?" he said. "These guys get everything they want handed to them. They just received a pay increase, they wanted to wear new uniform shirts which I approved it, and they are driving around in a new apparatus. We are the envy of every department in the county and not one of them wants to get involved in anything."

As the admin chief listened to her boss complain, all she could think of was how disconnected this chief was with the members of his organization. His department membership did want to get involved. In fact, they were involved. They fought tooth and nail to get that contract raise for three years. They fought for longer than that for permission from their chief to wear their new uniform shirts. And about a dozen of them were on the apparatus committee that was developed to design their new apparatus. They were very enthusiastic about being involved in the process; however, the apparatus they ended up receiving was not the one they designed, because the chief changed the specs in the fourth quarter and ended up ordering a completely different rig than the one the committee designed with no explanation other that the fact that he wanted something different.

The apparatus debacle was the last straw for the members. They felt as if they'd wasted their time and were disrespected by the chief. In return for the way they were treated, they collectively decided not to volunteer to do anything more than the minimum requirements to keep their jobs.

That story describes a controlling micromanager with the mindset of, "It's my department, you'll follow my rules, and you will do it the way I tell you to do it. If not, there will be consequences."

I once met with a handful of firefighters from a fire department outside of Houston Texas, they told me how happy they were with their management and executive officers.

"There is no ego, hidden agendas and no micro-managing," one of them said. "They (the administrative staff) listen to us, involve us in decisions, give us meaningful assignments, and treat us with respect. We are all very blessed to be working here."

Which one of the two organizations described above would you rather work for?

Micromanagers stifle initiative and frustrate employees.

Micromanagers stifle initiative and frustrate employees. They do this by constantly looking over the shoulders of their subordinates and team members and trying to get them to do things the way they would do it. Do not do this to your team members. If their way is working, and it is an ethical, acceptable practice, let them run with it. Do not misinterpret this message. If someone on your team is clearly doing something incorrectly, you absolutely should correct them. The mistake many people in leadership positions make, however, is they think it is their job to always be looking for what people are doing wrong. When you treat your team members like they are children, they will tend to do less. If you praise people for what they do right, they will tend to do more. This is a simple principle of human nature. People like to be praised and rewarded for good behavior and activity, and they shy away from people who constantly criticize, condemn, and complain.

Every workplace needs structure and leadership, but a rigid, top-down organization that does not enable people to learn, grow, and contribute ideas makes for unhappy employees. If your best performers are expected to produce results without ever being allowed to express their concerns, or if they are not empowered to make decisions, or if they are constantly having to defer important jobs to their supervisors because of their title, even when they are perfectly capable and willing to accomplish a specific task themselves, they are not left with much to be happy about.

Many people who leave their job do so because of their boss, not the work or the organization. More than eighty percent of Americans feel they work for a micromanager. That is a remarkably high number. Perhaps this is a sign of insecurity because some people feel that strong, competent employees are a threat to their position or authority as opposed to a complement to their weakness.

The National Football League's New England Patriots, from 2000 until 2019, will forever be considered one of America's longest-running and most dominant dynasties. During that time frame, the Patriots played in eight consecutive AFC Championship games (between 2011 and 2018), appeared in nine Super Bowls, and won six. They also recorded nineteen consecutive winning seasons, including one undefeated sixteen-game regular season. During this era, two men, head coach Bill Belichick and quarterback Tom Brady, are consistently credited with the Patriots' success by helping to create a sustainable culture around the team. Their emphasis of that culture, dubbed the Patriot Way, was placed on personal accountability, consistent improvement, and a focus on the team success over personal gain.

One of the mottos the Patriots have become famous for is: "Do your job." Notice that it does not read: "Do your job the way I would do it." The point is that during that time, Belichick and the Patriots organization did a great job at bringing in talented individuals, putting them in the right position, and requiring that they do their job on the field. If everyone knew their job and did their job, the team would succeed.

Leaders need to understand the importance of layered leadership, which is the need to have leaders throughout their organization. Belichick understood the importance of putting the right people in the right position and letting them do their job. Would the Patriots have been as successful as they were if the coach did not allow his players to do their job on the field the way they knew how to? The likely answer is no.

Roger Thomas Staubach, also known as Roger the Dodger, Captain America, and Captain Comeback, played quarterback for the Dallas Cowboys for eleven years after signing with the franchise in 1969. During that time frame, Staubach was named to the Pro Bowl six times and led his team to five Super Bowls in which he won two. He was named Most Valuable Player of Super Bowl VI, becoming the first player to win both the Heisman Trophy and Super Bowl MVP awards. Before becoming a professional football player, Staubach attended the U.S. Naval Academy. His coach, Wayne Harding, recognized that Staubach played with a style and natural instinct that could not be taught, so he did what any great manager should do – put the right person in the right position, supported him, and got out of his way.

Micromanaging kills trust and stifles initiative, yet many people still tend to do it without realizing that they are. I would even place myself in that category. When my middle son was nine-years-old, I brought him for a pitching lesson from a former Major League Baseball player. My intent was simple. My son was pitching for his little league team, and he was doing well, but I wanted to make sure that I was not allowing him to develop any bad habits. Although I played baseball when I was younger, it was not my primary sport, and I was not a pitcher. When I had written my first book, I was still typing with four fingers – and I am not kidding. To this day, I still do not type correctly, even though I did graduate to seven fingers. I had never learned to type correctly. In rare occurrences, one of my pinkies somehow finds and hits a key. (Do not feel bad for me, this is my ninth published book). The point I am making is that I have developed a bad habit that is still with me to this day, and the reason why I brought my son for a pitching lesson was because I did not want this same thing to happen to him.

The coach took his time with my son and explained to me all the things he was doing correct. His mechanics were good, and he was a lefty with natural movement on the ball.

"That's going to be a tough pitch for a nine-year-old to hit," the coach said. "The main goal is to throw strikes. At this age, you do not want to mess around with pitches or try to hit corners. All you want from your pitchers, is to not walk the game away."

"Is there anything we should change?" I asked.

"Well, he holds the ball with two seams. I would switch that to four seams," he said while showing me the exact way he wanted me to have my son grip the ball. Then he continued with, "But I wouldn't worry about that yet. He is still young, and his hand is small. Let him continue doing what he is doing, and you can work on this when he gets a little older."

Two days later, I brought my son out to throw about twenty-five pitches, which we would do a few times a week. After he warmed up and threw a handful of pitches, I told him to switch to four seams.

"But, Dad, I don't like the way that feels," he said.

"That's only because it's new, but you'll get used to it," I explained.

Although he continued to protest with each pitch, I would not let him switch back to two seams. My thought was that I wanted him to get ahead of the curve with this so he could continue progressing and not fall behind. The problem was that my son had a difficult time throwing a strike. After throwing about fifteen consecutive balls, I gave in and told him he could switch back to two seams. He immediately began throwing strikes again. Then it hit me. The coach, when talking about switching to four seams, had said, *"I wouldn't worry about that yet. He is still young, and his hand is small. Let him continue doing what he is doing, and you can work on this when he gets a little older."*

I also considered his comments about throwing strikes being the main goal. Instead of focusing on the fact that my son was accomplishing that goal, I started to micromanage his process, which in turn caused him to lose the strike zone and fail to do what a nine-year-old pitcher needed to do – throw strikes.

More than eighty percent of Americans feel they work for a micromanager.

If you have micromanaging tendencies, fear not. There is a simple three-step solution that can help you overcome this problem.

1. Manage the outcome, not the process.

Everyone has their own process for doing things. If an individual or team is producing the results you want, and they are doing it in a legal, ethical, acceptable way, do not be so quick to change the way they do things just because you would do it a different way.

2. Put people in the right position based on their talent, skills & ability.

When you put your aces in their places, you will be less likely to look over their shoulders and micromanage their methods. When you have competent team members, be smart enough to take advantage of that luxury.

3. Delegate with the intentions of developing your team members.

Use delegation as a tool to help develop your team members. Give people assignments that will help them grow and improve. By doing so, you will increase the number of competent people you will have on your team to choose from.

You are in the people business. Your number one asset must be your team members. Your job is to inspire and empower them. Many organizations are obsessed with mission statements, but not enough of them have a *permission* statement, such as, "We give our employees permission to act." There will be times when people do things incorrectly, and yes, you must correct them. Do so in a respectful manner. Most people do not mind being criticized, but no one likes being minimized.

It is important to bring people with the right attitude and skill set onto your team. Many CEO's would agree that a high percent of the success their organization had achieved was derived from bringing the right people onto the team. That said, you have the responsibility to develop all your people to be able to excel in a variety of situations. One of the best ways to do this is through effective delegation.

How To Delegate

Dividing tasks and developing your people multiplies your chances of success. Do not be fooled into thinking that delegation is the simple act of passing your responsibilities on to someone else. As sure as there are rewards for proper delegation, there are absolute consequences for improper delegation. For team leaders to delegate effectively they should first feel secure about their own position and understand the strengths and weaknesses of those around them. Here are the six steps to effective delegation.

1. Establish and maintain an environment that is favorable to delegating.

This begins by creating team spirit. You are one team, with one mission. Everyone should understand that they all have a role to play in the overall success or failure of the mission. As the team leader, you must clearly understand the tasks you are delegating, and you must be able to articulate the reasons why each task is important. If the "what" and "why" are not clear in your own mind, you will not be able to effectively communicate the mission with others. You must also take into consideration the resources that are available to you and the timeline in which the task needs to be accomplished.

When delegating assignments, be prepared to express the importance of the task, the desired results, the available resources, the acceptable practices, the time frame in which you want it completed by, and, of course, your confidence in the person(s) you have selected. At this point, you are ready to delegate; however, do not lose sight of the fact that when you delegate, you are not relinquishing responsibility. As the leader, you are still ultimately responsible for the overall project.

2. Select the right person for the job.

It cannot be stressed enough that when you know what your team members' strengths and limitations are, you will have an easier time delegating properly. Ideally, the person chosen to tackle a task should have the talent, skills, ability, knowledge, enthusiasm, and time needed to get the job done. If you have a difficult time finding the right person, contemplate the answers to questions such as:

•   Who is best equipped to handle this job?

- Who accepts challenges and is likely to rise to the occasion?

- Can one person do this job, or will it require multiple team members?

- Does the task require previous experience, or is training needed?

- Who would learn the most by accepting this responsibility?

- Who would benefit the least if assigned this task?

- Who can I trust to do the job?

3. Ensure that the person accepting the assignment understands it.

When giving the assignment, encourage the delegate to ask questions so you can eliminate any confusion. Also be sure to express how much authority you are handing over. You may choose to provide guidance by saying something like, "Look into the problem, suggest a few possible solutions, and together we will choose the best one." Or you may have enough confidence in that individual to say, "Solve the problem and let me know what actions you have taken." The person to whom you are delegating the task should not only have a clear picture of what you want, they should also be aware that by accepting the assignment, he or she is taking a positive step forward because they are proving to be a competent and valuable member of your organization.

4. Keep an open-door policy.

The lines of communication should always remain open. Let the delegate know he or she should not hesitate to ask for help. Make yourself available to provide the individual with assistance if needed.

If the task or project is one that will take several days, weeks, or even months to accomplish, acquire periodic progress reports to make sure this project is moving forward. When you meet to exchange information, it would most likely not need to be for more than a few minutes. Your focus should be to find out what has been accomplished, what still needs to be accomplished, what problems have been encountered, and what resources are needed to complete the assignment.

5. Be prepared to accept and deal with the consequences of that person's actions if he or she does not meet your organization's expectations.

Make sure everyone on your team fully understood that you have their backs if things unexpectedly went wrong. . This does not mean that you must lower your standards and accept less than their best effort. It simply means that when honest mistakes are made, you will approach the situation with a level head and take into consideration the fact that you assigned this task to this individual because you felt he or she was competent. No one comes to work thinking, "Today I really want to mess up." An unsatisfactory outcome could be a result of situations that are out of the individual's control. Since you delegated the assignment to a person you have confidence in, that individual deserves your support before jumping to conclusions.

6.   Always reward performance.

Reward and recognition are vitally important when it comes to expressing appreciation. The people who voluntarily work the hardest are often those who feel the most appreciated. It is your responsibility to show appreciation for a job well done by recognizing quality work privately and publicly. The level of appreciation you feel for another person is not important if you do not show it to them. What is important is how appreciated *they* feel. Sincere recognition will increase your effectiveness in keeping team morale high. Do not reward hard-working team members by consistently giving them more work than you give to others. Although that is a sign of respect for a competent individual, it is also poor management to put so much work on one person's shoulders that you fail to help develop the skills of others on the team. Consciously work to empower others in such a way that they help develop and execute your ideas, and you will become significantly more efficient than you would have become by doing it all yourself.

The purpose of delegating is not to avoid work or unload difficult or tedious tasks on others. Effective delegation is an absolute necessity when it comes to a team's success. When you divide tasks, you multiply your chances of success. Many companies spend tens of thousands, if not hundreds of thousands of dollars on new technology, equipment, or vehicles, but they don't spend a fraction of that cost on developing the people who will be using the new technology, equipment, or vehicles.

You need to invest in your people, and you can do that through training and delegation. Failure to delegate will result in a failure to adequately develop your team. Through delegation, your team will grow in confidence. They, and your entire organization, will benefit in the long run. A CFO once asked a CEO: "What happens if we invest in developing our people and they leave us?" The CEO replied with, "What happens if we do not invest in our people, and they stay?"

> ## Dividing tasks and developing your people multiplies your chances of success.

With all this information on why delegation is the proper way to run an organization, you may be wondering why more people do not do it? Some may not do it because they see delegation as a sign of weakness. Others hesitant to delegate because they feel they can do everything better themselves. Perhaps some do not want anyone else making decisions, or they do not like receiving feedback from others, or they are too busy having meetings where they tell everyone what they are doing wrong. These are all signs of what you do not want to become – the classic micromanager.

Chapter Recap

combustible tips to ignite your team

Take the time to develop your people. One of the best ways to do that is though effective delegation. Delegating tasks does not mean you are passing your responsibilities on to other people. It simply means that you recognize that you have talent all around you and you understand the value of putting the right people in the right positions. You also understand the value in putting people in situations where they can fail, learn, grow, and improve. Everyone plays a role in helping to prepare the people on their team. You have probably already heard the phrase "It takes a village to raise a child." It also takes a village to raise a competent, contributing team member. Unfortunately, some people who may be capable of doing the more difficult tasks choose to criticize those who cannot. Then there are those who are capable, and talented, who choose to take the time to help teach those who struggle. The latter are the best people to have in your organization. They are the ones who will help your team reach the fully developed stage of team development.

5

HAVE THE GUTS TO PERSIST

*At some point in a fight, technique gives way
to heart and determination.*

As a young actor, Sylvester Stallone used to spend a lot of time in his apartment that was so small he was able to open the window and close the door while sitting on his bed. Although his living space was limited, it was private with little to no distractions. Stallone would take advantage of this privacy by sitting in his bed, with a pen and legal pad, and writing short stories. One of the subjects that continued to reoccur in his stories was the concept of unrealized dreams. He was attracted to tales about the down-on-his-luck drifter who never got his shot, or the person who never gave up even though the deck was stacked against him. These themes resonated with Stallone, who was struggling to find work as an actor and having a hard time paying the bills. Things became so tight that he eventually had to sell his dog just to get by.

One March 24, 1975, Stallone went to see a title fight between legendary professional boxing champion Muhammad Ali and New Jersey's Chuck Wepner. Wepner was such an enormous underdog that many people thought he should not have even been given the title fight. Stallone referred to Wepner as a stumblebum; however, about halfway through round 9, Ali threw a jab. Wepner slipped under it and threw a big right hook under the heart of Ali, knocking him down to the canvas. This was only the third time in Ali's career that he was knocked down. For a moment, the underdog stumblebum rose to the challenge and earned the respect he rightfully deserved. Most of those in attendance were shocked by the unexpected turn of events. Many of them began cheering for Wepner. The fight went into the 15th round before Ali won by TKO, but the night belonged to Wepner because his entire life's journey crystallized at that moment. He would be immortalized and remembered by fight fans forever as the underdog who refused to go down without a fight.

For Stallone, the fight was a metaphor for life. It was also the catalyst he needed for an idea: the man who is going to stand up to life, take one shot, and maybe – just maybe – go the distance. He started writing. The words flew out of his pen and onto his legal pad for three straight days until he completed the script for *Rocky*.

Shortly after writing the script, Stallone attended a casting call and auditioned for a roll in an upcoming film that was being produced by Irwin Winkler and Robert Chartoff. He was not right for the part; however, before he left, Stallone mentioned that he also does a bit of writing and had been working on a story about a boxer. The producers told him to bring it around sometime, which he did, and they quickly became enthusiastic about the story. They wanted to purchase the script, but they did not want Stallone to star in it. They offered him $25,000 for the story rights, but Stallone declined the offer. At the time he did not blame them for not wanting to use him as the main character. He was unknown and unproven, but something inside made him realize the opportunity to star as Rocky would never come around again, so he declined the offer to sell the story. The producers then increased their offer to $100,000. Stallone had $160 in the bank at the time. His car had just broken down and he had already sold his dog, but again he passed on the offer. They raised it to $150K, then $175K, then $250K. At this point, his head was spinning. He had never seen that much money, but his gut continued to tell him to decline the offers. When the offer came in for $330K, the decision was not so easy; however, Stallone began thinking about how he had been able to manage poverty. He felt he had it down to a science in the sense that he did not need much to live on. He passed once again. The offer went as high as $360K. That is when Stallone told himself that if he were to sell the rights to the script without being able to play the part of Rocky, and the movie did well, he would be devastated because he firmly believed that he should play the part of Rocky. He decided to continue to roll the dice, and it paid off.

Eventually, they bought the script and made the movie with Sylvester Stallone starring as Rocky Balboa. In 1976, *Rocky* hit the theaters and moviegoers loved it. The film won an Oscar for Best Picture and Stallone went on to become one of the biggest action movie stars of all time.

Stallone had often praised Winkler and Chartoff for their insight, patience, and willingness to take a chance. But consider what would have happened if Stallone had not stopped on his way out of that audition and mentioned that he was also a writer? And what would have become of the actor if he had sold the script for the original offer of $25,000 and they casted someone else to play the lead character?

For Stallone, it was all about holding on tight to his dream. Like his fictional character Rocky Balboa, Stallone had been humbled and knocked down by life, but he continued to take the types of blows that people who are chasing their dream often encounter and kept moving forward until he was victorious.

Many people contemplate throwing in the towel when things get tough, and some do. Many successful people have considered quitting things that ended up becoming their greatest achievements. There will be times when you feel like it might not happen. During those times, it is okay to have moments of weakness and doubt, but do not give up on your dreams. The key for many people who have overcome adversity in their life has been to take the blows and keep moving forward.

Find The Road to "Yes"

You may know me as an established author who has written a few bestsellers. If so, thank you for having enough belief in me to pick up and read this book. I hope you find value and encouragement on these pages, and I believe that you will when you read the following story about how I became an author. I was not an author who became a firefighter. I was a firefighter who became inspired to write after 9/11. Yes, that 9/11.

When the first plane struck the world trade center and the news came on television screens across America, I ran outside of my fire station on Midland Avenue in Kearny, New Jersey, and looked at the towers to see if this was really happening. The Town of Kearny is located a few miles away from Manhattan. Kearny is a neighboring town of Jersey City, and my fire station is on top of a hill, which offered a clear, unobstructed view of the Manhattan skyline.

After the second plane hit, and it became apparent that this was a terrorist attack on our country, most of our members were called in to protect our community. On the following day, a six-team task force consisting of thirty-two firefighters from my department headed over to Manhattan to assist in the rescue and recovery effort. When I first arrived at ground zero, it took about an hour for the whole scene to sink in. This is the most horrific disaster we will ever see in our lives, and I was standing right there, in the middle of it. There was thick white concrete dust covering every inch of the ground as we walked toward the site. Usually, a group of thirty or so firefighters walking down a street together is comical and entertaining. They would be telling stories and ripping on each other, but this day we were silent. I began to take note of what I was seeing. There were police officers, EMS workers, and steelworkers scattered throughout the streets, but as we stood a block from the pile waiting for our assignment we were surrounded by hundreds of uniformed firefighters. Although the names on their helmet shields were different, that day we all worked for Team USA. It did not take long before we were directed to move toward Ground Zero, and in the blink of an eye I found myself standing on top of an enormous mountain of broken concrete and twisted steel. It was surreal to think that this pile of debris was the remains of the Twin Towers, but there we were, in a bucket brigade with hundreds of brother and sister firefighters, passing full buckets down and moving empty ones back up, hoping to find any sign of life.

There are a few moments in your life that change who you are as a person. One of those moments was when my first son was born. I am sure most parents would agree that something inside of you changes when you bring a life into the world. It certainly changed for me, because for the first time in my life I realized that I truly was living for a reason much bigger than myself. Another one of those moments happened on the day that I was standing on top of a pile of steel and concrete that two days earlier was a symbol for American pride, strength, and excellence.

Now, I must admit, the change in me did not happen immediately, it took a few weeks, but for the first time in my life I had come to realize that I was not living the life I wanted to live. Many of the decisions I'd made up to that point were based on self-doubt. Although I had ambition, I seemed to always find a reason why I would fail to achieve the goals I was setting for myself. Part of this was because I still placed more value in other people's opinions of my worth and potential than I did in my own. I felt as if I'd built a self-containing cage using the limited expectation of other people's beliefs in my potential as the bars that kept me confined. Later in my life, a friend shared with me the twenty things a person should stop wearing: Numbers 1 through 20 were *the weight of other people's unrealistic expectations and judgments*. After what I had just experienced on the days that followed 9/11, those bars and that weight did not seem strong enough to be able to contain me anymore. My mindset had shifted from "I should be doing this but I'm not" to "I am going to do this because I have something to offer the world." I began to believe that my voice mattered, and my potential was far greater than I had previously realized.

One day, shortly after this mental shift, I was having lunch with a friend and co-worker when I shared something that had been on my mind.

"I'm going to write a book," I said.

"About what?" he asked.

"New Jersey firefighters," I replied.

I went on to explain how everyone would always know about the sacrifices the firefighters made on 9/11, but no one would ever know about the sacrifices so many firefighters in our state had made, unless someone shared those stories.

My buddy admitted it was a good idea, but I could see the skepticism in his face, and for good reason. He and I went to high school together. Let me just say that he graduated in the top half of our class. I, on the other hand, graduated in the half that made the top half possible.

In retrospect, I am certain that the best thing I did that day was share my intentions with my buddy. By doing so, I made myself accountable. This is something I had not done much of in the past, so once I put it out there, I felt empowered.

The next morning, I purchased a tape recorder, called a firefighter I knew from a nearby town who'd received an award for making a rescue, and asked if I could interview him for a book that I was writing. He agreed to meet, but he also stressed that what happened on that day was no big deal and probably not worthy of being shared in a book.

On the day we met, I turned on my tape recorder and asked him to share what happened. As he told me the story, I realized he was wrong. This story absolutely had to be told, and I was excited to be the one to tell it. The next morning, I turned on my computer, and started to type. It took me about three minutes to realize I was in over my head. Although I was able to visualize the incident happening in my mind, I could not figure out how to transfer what I was seeing into the written word in a way that captured the spirit of the story. After a couple days of what some authors would refer to as writer's block, I decided to visit my local bookstore to find some inspiration and ended up purchasing a book on the topic of how to write a book. I read and continuously referred to that book over the next few months as I interviewed more than twenty firefighters and transferred their experiences into the written word.

Six months after conceiving the idea to write the book, I had completed the manuscript for *Common Valor: True Stories from America's Bravest: Volume 1*. Now I needed to figure out how to get it published. Seeking guidance, I went back to the bookstore and purchased another book on thew topic of getting your book published. Early in that book, the author suggested that an aspiring author would need to get an agent because most publishing companies do not accept unsolicited manuscripts. This was a couple years before the internet was widely known or developed, so the next thing I did was return to the bookstore again to purchase a book that provided names and contact information of credible literary agents throughout the country.

I highlighted about fifty agents who were looking to represent authors of nonfiction books and sent the majority of them sample chapters along with a query letter and included a self-addressed stamped envelope so I could receive their response to the question "Would you be interested in representing me?"

Over the next few weeks, I received a consistent flow of replies that all echoed the same reply of, "Not at this time." It was becoming abundantly clear to me that this was not going to happen anytime soon. The old me would have thrown in the towel, but I had come too far to do that, so I contemplated my next move and realized that I had to be my own biggest advocate. I had to find my road to yes. If I could not secure an agent, it was no big deal. The way I looked at, all the agent was going to do was introduce me to the publisher and broker the deal, so I decided I was going to represent myself.

I began to implement the six degrees of separation concept, which posits that any two people on the Earth are six or fewer acquaintances apart. I may not know anyone who works for a publishing company, but someone I know must know someone who does.

> ## 20 things you should stop wearing – Numbers 1 through 20: the weight of other people's unrealistic expectations and judgments.

While sitting at my office desk, contemplating whom to call, my eyes drifted across the room and landed on an issue of *Firehouse Magazine*. I picked it up, began thumbing through it, and saw the name of the editor, Harvey Eisner. Although I did not know Mr. Eisner, I had heard from multiple people that he was a great guy who served for many years as a New Jersey firefighter. Since my book was about New Jersey firefighters, I thought this would be the perfect person to call for advice. I called directory assistance and acquired the number for his office. After three rings, a man picked up.

"Hello, this is Harvey Eisner."

"Mr. Eisner?" I asked. Mostly because I was not expecting him to pick up and needed to buy a few moments to gather my thoughts.

"Yes," he replied.

"Hello. My name is Frank Viscuso. I am a fire captain from Kearny, New Jersey, and I had written a book about New Jersey firefighters, and I was wondering if *Firehouse Magazine* published books, or if you knew anyone who does."

"We do not, but I do know someone who does," he replied. After a wonderful ten-minute conversation with Mr. Eisner, he gave me a publisher's phone number and told me to tell the man that Harvey had given me his number. That man ended up publishing my first book.

Like Stallone, I often wonder what would have happened if I did not take the chance to make this call and ask that question. Great things can happen when you take a chance. To date I have nine published books. Several of them have been Amazon best-sellers. I also have a few unpublished manuscripts and a handful of screenplays that may be of interest to someone in the film and television industries one day.

What is that you are trying to accomplish. Perhaps you would like to write a book. Maybe you are trying to get a promotion at work, win a championship, or close that big deal. Whatever it is, make the decision that you are going to be determined enough to overcome whatever adversity you encounter, continue to move forward, persist, and find the road to yes.

"We Didn't Come Here to Punt!"

National Football League Quarterback Jim McMahon led the Chicago Bears to a dominant 46–10 win over the New England Patriots in Super Bowl XX following the 1985 season. Five years before reaching the pinnacle of success in his sport, McMahon was the quarterback of the Brigham Young University football team. As a sophomore, he replaced starting quarterback Marc Wilson after Wilson suffered an injury. McMahon stepped up to the challenge and displayed confidence and tenacity from the moment he was assigned to his new leadership role. This did not come as a surprise to anyone who knew him since McMahon was known for his tenacity; the level of which was never more evident than in the 1980 Holiday Bowl.

With only four minutes left in the game, BYU was down by 20 points. When they failed to convert a first down around the midfield, head coach LaVell Edwards sent his punting unit onto the field. Baffled by the call, McMahon refused to come out. Instead, the quarterback sent the punter off the field and told his offense to stay on. Edwards called a time out. McMahon was livid as he approached his coach on the sideline. With rising emotion, McMahon voiced his displeasure about the call.

Realizing how upset and convicted McMahon was, Edwards allowed his quarterback to go for the first down. In the huddle, McMahon told his team that they did not come all this way to punt the ball. He called a play. BYU converted the fourth down, then immediately scored a touchdown, followed by another, and another on the last play with a Hail Mary pass to the end zone. McMahon and his offense scored 21 unanswered points in the final few minutes and won the game.

American sports history is full of great examples of guts and tenacity like that one. Kerri Strug's achievement in the 1996 Summer Olympics is one of them. Strug was a member of the women's gymnastics team that represented the United States that summer. The team, which had come to be known as the Magnificent Seven, consisted of Strug, Shannon Miller, Dominique Moceanu, Dominique Dawes, Amy Chow, Amanda Borden, and Jaycie Phelps. The performances that these women entertained the world with earned the United States its first ever all-around gold medal in the women's team competition. Although Miller, Dawes, and Chow also won individual medals, the most memorable performance by any team member during the '96 Olympics in Atlanta that year came from Strug in the vault competition.

After compulsories, Strug was ranked 9th overall and had qualified to complete in the event finals for both the floor exercise and the vault. In the team competition, the United States was up against the Ukrainian, Romanian and Russian teams. The Russians, who had dominated the team competition for decades, had entered the final stage of the Olympic competition with a slight lead. On the final day, the U.S. gained some momentum and took a strong 0.897-point lead over the Russian team. The event came down to the final rotation, with the Russians on floor exercise and the U.S. on vault. If the U.S. team continued performing the way they had been, they would surely walk away as the victors, however, their first four gymnasts failed to land their vaults cleanly, resulting in low scores, leaving Strug as the final vaulter for the United States.

In her first attempt, Strug continued the string of bad luck for the Americans by under-rotating the landing, causing her to fall and injure her ankle. She was given a score of 9.162 points. Strug would need to land her second vault on her feet for the U.S. to clinch the Gold Medal. Immediately after her failed vault, and moments before her last attempt, Strug turned to her coach, Béla Károlyi, and asked, "Do we need this?"

"Kerri, we need you to go one more time. We need you one more time for the Gold. You can do it, you better do it," Károlyi replied.

Strug limped onto the runway and prepared for her second attempt. She took a deep breath, ran down the runway, performed her vault, and stuck the landing on both feet, before instantly hopping on her good foot. Strug saluted the judges before collapsing onto her knees and being assisted off the landing platform. Her vault received a score of 9.712, guaranteeing the Americans the gold medal and making Strug a national sports hero for her display of grit and tenacity.

Most Americans who watched the '96 Olympics would remember the image of Coach Béla Károlyi carrying his injured warrior onto the medals podium to join her team. Strug was later treated at the hospital for third-degree lateral sprain and tendon damage. She was unable to complete in the individual all-around competition and event finals, but her heroic performance on that day captured the hearts and earned the admiration of every American.

Grit and Perseverance

You are obviously reading this book because you are interested in achieving a higher level of success in your chosen field. Hopefully, you have set your expectations high and are mapping out your game plan. The challenge with high expectations is that they come with a high risk of potential failure, and most people would prefer to remain in their comfort zone. By now, you have more than likely come to the realization that no one has ever achieved success in their comfort zone.

The next time you are in a roomful of colleagues, look around and pick the person who has achieved the highest level of success. You will likely be looking at a person who has mastered specific skills and established productive daily habits, but there is also strong possibility that you will be looking at the person who has also failed the most.

Talent is a wonderful thing, but this world is full of talented people who lack fortitude and determination. Steve Jobs once said, "I'm convinced that about half of what separates the successful entrepreneurs from the unsuccessful ones is pure perseverance." Perseverance is defined as steadfastness in doing something despite difficulty or delay in achieving success. The word perseverance is often interchangeable with another word—Grit. Grit is "the great equalizer." Many people with natural talent and ability have crossed finish lines in business and sports behind others who had less talent, but more grit and perseverance.

> Talent is a wonderful thing, but this world is full of talented people who lack fortitude and determination.

In her TED talk titled "Grit: The Power of Passion and Perseverance," author Angela Lee Duckworth shared an experience she had after leaving a demanding management consulting job at the age of twenty-seven to take a position as a seventh-grade math teacher in the New York City public school system—a position she quickly discovered was even more demanding than her previous job. After calculating grades, she realized that IQ was not the only difference between her best and worst academic students. Some of her strongest performers did not have high IQ scores and some of her smartest kids were not able to keep up their GPAs. This led Duckworth to contemplate the thought that, within our educational system, the one thing we know how to measure best is IQ, but what if doing well in school and in life depends on much more than a person's ability to learn quickly and easily.

Duckworth ended up leaving the classroom to continue her own education in graduate school, and eventually became a psychologist. She began studying the performance of kids and adults in super challenging settings, which included students at West Point Military Academy as well as adults in highly competitive sales markets. In every study, she and her team sought the answer to one simple question: "Who is successful, and why?"

What she discovered is that one characteristic consistently emerged as a significant predictor of success. It was not social intelligence, good looks, physical health, or IQ. It was grit. Grit is defined as courage and resolve, strength of character. Duckworth describes grit as perseverance and passion for very long-term goals.

In 2018, *Fortune* magazine posted an article titled "Grit is the new MBA." In the article, the author featured six executives who developed the skills and grittiness that helped them reach the pinnacle of success in their careers by providing them with the tools needed to overcome complex challenges early in their life. The author listed four professions where grit matters most, and among them was public servants, and for good reason. One would be hard pressed to name a profession that requires more grittiness than that of a firefighter, paramedic, or police officer. Many of the people who are attracted to these professions already have this characteristic, which is a good thing since grit is a transferrable quality. Meaning: a person who has demonstrated the ability to overcome challenges in one area is likely to draw from that experience when needed in other areas of life.

What about those who do not have that type of gritty stamina? Can they develop it? One man who knows the true meaning of the word *grit* is former Navy SEAL and endurance athlete David Goggins. Goggins is the only member of the United States Armed Forces to complete SEAL training,

Army Ranger School, *and* the Airforce Tactical Air Controller training. Goggins also competed in numerous ultramarathons, including hundred-mile races that have pushed his mind and body to the absolute limit. From the outside looking in, one would think that a person who has accomplished what Goggins has, must have superior genetics, but in one podcast interview, Goggins set the record straight by saying, "I'm not the best at anything. I'm not gifted. I'm just driven." He grew up with some of the same types of self-limiting insecurities that many people have, but he developed his mind to believe that it is possible to excel in the face of adversity.

To build his grittiness, the former SEAL began to do the things every day that he did not want to do, like run in the cold and in the rain. He advised listeners to run when they do not feel like running and push themselves further then they believed they can go. Goggins stated that when most people's minds are telling them that they are finished, they are probably only about 40 percent done. He compares the mind to a governor that is put on a car engine to prevent it from going faster.

We all have limitations, but most of us would never know what we are truly capable of until we pushed ourselves to those places that we did not know we could go. I worked with a company officer who is a certified personal trainer, and he understood the connection between mental and physical performance. He also understood the value of incorporating physical fitness into training when performing essential job skills. I once observed a "combat ready" drill that he set up for the members of our team.

The drill began with the two-minute donning drill in which each firefighter had to don their full turnout gear (bunker gear, hood, gloves, SCBA, PASS alarm, etc.) until they were ready to enter the structure, and be on-air, in less than two minutes. Immediately after completing this task, the firefighter would grab an axe and Halligan bar, then climb up and down four flights of stairs to work up their heart rate. The firefighter would then deploy a hose line which was connected to the pumper, remove the nozzle, add an additional length, and reconnect the nozzle to the end of the hose to simulate "piecing in." The next step would be to fully advance the hose line. After completing this task, the firefighter would drag a 160-pound rescue manikin fifty-feet to safety, then perform a reduced profile maneuver (by removing his or her SCBA) to fit between two studs to end the drill. After completing the exercise, the other members of the team did the same. Afterward, the officer shared their times, and they discussed ways to improve. It should be noted that this exercise was conducted after previously training for two hours on other essential firefighting skills.

The goal was simple: build the body and mind together while learning the skills needed to achieve success in their field. Push yourself during training so when you need to perform in a high-pressure situation you are equipped with knowledge as well as strong mental and physical conditioning.

You may be in a field where you do not have to conduct the type of training this officer did to develop a team that performs well under pressure, but I would suggest that you make a conscious effort to become uncommon. Do not allow complacency to set up camp in your workplace. We live in a society that often rewards mediocrity. Gritty people detest mediocrity. My hope for you is that you strive for something more than mediocrity.

> Do not allow complacency to set up camp in your workplace.

By the end of the 2020 season, Rutgers head wrestling coach Scott Goodale was the winningest coach in program history, with 183 career victories. Since taking over the program on July 31, 2007, Coach Goodale and his staff had turned Rutgers wrestling into one of the most relevant teams in the country. During that time frame, the Scarlet Knights had produced two individual national champions, five individual conference titles, and fifteen All-Americans. Between 2009 and 2019, the team earned two Top 10 finishes and eight Top 25 finishes in the USA Today / NWCA Division I Coaches Poll.

The 2018–19 campaign was the best in the program's eighty-nine-year history up to that point, as Rutgers recorded its first Top 10 finish at the NCAA Championships with its ninth-place result on March 23, 2019, in Pittsburgh. The performance was highlighted by individual national titles for Nick Suriano (133 pounds) and Anthony Ashnault (149 pounds), and Goodale was named NCAA Tournament Coach of the Year.

During an interview on *Flashpoint: The Fire Inside Podcast*, I asked Coach Goodale what he does to teach and promote toughness and aggressiveness in his wrestlers. He explained how his staff likes to create strenuous and challenging situations at practice so the wrestlers will be better equipped to overcome challenges against their opponents. This, once again, goes back to how a team trains and prepares. Wrestling is certainly a sport where grit and the ability to persist are as important tactical superiority. Legendary American wrestler and coach Dan Gable said it best with his words, "The 1st period is won by the best technician. The 2nd period is won by the kid in the best shape. The 3rd period is won by the kid with the biggest heart."

Heart and determination may be tucked away deep inside the bodies of some of your team members and it may stay there unless you find a way to bring it out. My department had once legally acquired a vacant warehouse to train in prior to its demolition. A dozen members of my crew were on site conducting multiple simultaneous wall-breaching drills when the captain of one of the crews told his newest recruit to come up and open one of the walls with an axe. The recruit stepped up, grabbed the axe, and began poking at the wall. The captain watched for a moment then asked the recruit to step back, which he did. The captain then turned to one of his seasoned veterans and said, "Show him."

The firefighter he was speaking with took the axe, stepped up, and began smashing the wall, quickly breaching a hole large enough for a firefighter to get through. The captain then looked at the recruit and calmly said, "That's what I want you to do."

Back at the fire station, the captain sat the recruit down to explain why toughness, effort, and aggressiveness is essential in our profession. Not arbitrary aggression, but rather intellectual and disciplined aggression – knowing when, why, and how to be aggressive. Author, clinical psychologist, and professor emeritus at the University of Toronto Dr. Jordan Peterson said, "You should be a monster, an absolute monster, and then you should learn how to control it."

Although aggressiveness and perseverance are two different things, they often go hand in hand, and they are usually the things that separate successful and unsuccessful people. Perseverance is about heart and determination and intestinal fortitude. It is about having the courage to play in pain, because sometimes in life you have no choice but to play in pain.

Courage is not always obvious. Yes, it takes courage to run into a burning building when others are running out, but that is not the type of courage a person needs to become a success in life. At the end of your life, your story will have been written. It is up to you if that story will include the words "I gave up" or the words "I fought until the end."

> "I'm convinced that about half of what separates the successful entrepreneurs from the non-successful ones is pure perseverance."
>
> – Steve Jobs

Embrace the Struggle

Success does not come without a price. That price will be different for everyone, but it will exist. Every great success story that you have ever witnessed, read about, or heard about has three components – the Dream, the Struggle, and the Victory. It all begins with a *Dream*, followed by a *Struggle*. Those who overcome their struggles move on to *Victory*. Those who cannot remain stuck, and many give up.

You must learn to embrace the struggle if you intend to reach the reward. Too many people want to stand on the peak, but they hate having to endure the strenuous climb it takes to get there. They want success, but they do not want to endure and overcome the struggle. That is where the problem lies. People want to grow, but they do not want to go through the growing pains.

> Too many people want to stand on the peak, but they hate having to endure the strenuous climb it takes to get there.

Too many quit during the struggle; and the struggle can be anything – Lack of time, lack of confidence, inability to overcome criticism, anything. A wise person will expect resistance every time he or she steps outside of their comfort zone. The sad part is that many people never start because they are anticipating hardship and struggle before they encounter it. It would benefit those people to discover that resistance, hardships, and struggles do not always break us, on the contrary, those are the exact things that usually help us become the people we are destined to become. I recall reading the following message that a friend posted on social media one day, "Everyone should be punched in the face at least once. Realizing you are not made of glass, and that it doesn't hurt as much as you feared it would, is extremely freeing." I certainly do not wish to see you get punched in the face, but the message he was conveying is a strong one.

Embrace the struggle. Every time you overcome a challenge you will become a better, stronger, more capable version of the individual you currently are. The same can be said for your team. One of the biggest reasons people and teams give up so fast is because they tend to look at how far they still need to go instead of how far they have already come.

Overcoming challenges requires endurance. Most of us have experienced the battle between the inner voice and the physical body. Take jogging for example. At some point in your life, you had made the decision that you needed to get in better shape. Perhaps you drove down to the local sporting goods store and bought some running shoes and a fancy jogging suit. You may have even purchased some sort of timer or downloaded a jogging app on your phone because you were fully committed to reaching your newly developed fitness goals. The next morning you woke up ready to tackle the day, so you went down to the local track, stretched out, and started running at a leisurely pace. You felt great for the first three minutes; however, at about the five-minute mark you realized how out of shape you actually were. Your heart started to resemble an escalating drum roll, droplets of sweat began rolling down your forehead, and a slight but troubling cramp decided to reside in your left hamstring. You were certain that you could deal with those issues because you had made a commitment, but then came the most unexpected problem of them all – self-pity.

That moment is the make-or-break point for most people. You must continue to remind yourself that your mind will quit before your body does. Deep down inside you know you can push through that initial mild wave of defeatism and continue running, but most people allow self-doubt to infiltrate their thinking to a point where it cripples their ability. This is the reason why so many pairs of running shoes are worn less than a dozen times. This is also the reason why gyms sell unlimited memberships even though they have a limited amount of square feet. When things get tough, most people quit.

You must learn how to defeat that increasingly insistent voice inside of your head that wants to keep you tucked warmly inside of that place known as your comfort zone – or what I like to refer to it as the *average* zone. Have you ever found yourself struggling with thoughts like, "I am not fast enough, or, I am not smart enough, or, I am not strong enough, or, I cannot do it, or, I am too late… too fat… too scared… too skinny… too ugly… too lazy, or, It's just too damn hard?" That is the voice you must learn how to defeat. When you conquer fear, self-doubt, and self-induced negativity, you will master your life. When you surround yourself with others who have done the same, you will have a team capable of achieving almost anything. Defeating that voice requires endurance, and endurance requires discipline.

Everybody wants to achieve something, but without a resilient work ethic and perseverance, nothing happens. You must have the intestinal fortitude to keep running when that voice is telling you that it is too hard. You must learn to embrace the struggle. Raw talent is a wonderful thing, but the world is full of talented underachievers who lack determination. Successful people train themselves to resist the urge to want to give up every time something becomes difficult.

Become a person who exemplifies the ability to persist and persevere. You do not have to be able to go forever. You just must be willing to go a little harder, and a little further than your competition. The number one reason people give up so fast is that they focus on how much further they need to go, instead of looking at how far they have come. They take their eyes off the prize and focus on the struggle. The struggle will be part of your journey. You cannot escape it. Embrace it because your successes and failures will be directly connected to your ability to persist and overcome the same types of challenges that would cause others to give up.

> Every time you overcome a challenge you will become a better, stronger, more capable version of the individual you currently are.

Critics and Toxic People
Time, Distance, and Shielding

Do you have critics?

Hopefully, you answered yes to that question. I am no stranger to criticism. In fact, the first time I taught at FDIC International in Indianapolis, Indiana,[1] I had come to realize that, like that seven-year-old travel baseball team mentioned earlier in this book, I was not fully prepared, and a couple of my reviews validated that fact. Two of my reviews were so bad that I wanted to fold them up, put them in my pocket, and make sure no one ever knew they existed.

---

[1] FDIC stands for Fire Department Instructors Conference, an annual conference and exhibition held at the Indiana Convention Center and Lucas Oil Stadium in Indianapolis, Indiana. It is one of the largest fire service conferences in the world, with more than 30,000 attendees.

That was a bad day.

Correction. That was a bad ten minutes that I expanded to 1,440 minutes. The next time you have a bad day, ask yourself, "Am I really having a bad day, or did I just have a moment that I let ruin the remainder of my day?"

Later that evening, I was waiting at the airport for my flight home when I started thinking about those reviews and wondering what my next step would be. Some of what those two individuals had written was true. For one thing, I did not feel as comfortable as I hoped I would when I stood in front of a room of my peers, so when one reviewer mentioned that I seemed reluctant, I agreed. Then it suddenly occurred to me that I was not teaching a class on the topic that I should be teaching on. I should have been teaching a class on leadership, team development, and customer service. Those were the topics I was passionate about. Those were the areas I had spent my adult life studying and working on developing. As a leader and coach in the fire service, business, and athletics, I knew what worked, and quite honestly what did not work. My past successes, and failures made me feel confident that I had something to say on those topics and I felt that I could make a difference. That night in the airport is when I conceived the idea to write the book *Step Up and Lead*, a book that continues to be one of the top selling leadership books in the fire service and has been referred to as the backbone of our industry.

Step Up and Lead was partially born out of a couple of bad reviews and some harsh criticism. By the way, I could have let those two reviews prevent me from submitting a proposal to speak at FDIC International the following year; however, I did not. In fact, my classrooms sold out each year that followed the release of my book, and less than ten years after those reviews, and I was honored to be selected as one of FDIC's opening ceremony keynote speakers.

You will have critics, but they will only have power over you if you give it to them, and you will continue to suffer if you have an emotional reaction to every negative comment that is ever said to you. Other people's opinions of you do not have to become your reality.

> Other people's opinions of you do not have to become your reality.

The world is full of critics. They are everywhere, in your neighborhood, your workplace, and sometimes even in your own household. And yes, they are even in the fire service. We have come to know them as the *Keyboard Commanders*. You know the ones I am talking about. They are the people who see a photo that was taken at a structure fire and blast the entire organization for their flawed tactics without knowing the full story of what they were up against the moment that photo was taken. Let me just write this once and be done with it. Firefighters need to stop criticizing their brothers and sisters on social media. No one is an expert at fighting the fires they were not at. When it comes to words like *empathy*, *teamwork*, and *camaraderie*, the men and women of fire service have set the bar for rest of society. Don't become the generation that destroys that reputation.

The people who are afraid to take the field are often the same ones who boo from the cheap seats. Sometimes, those boos come from internally. Toxic environments are created by toxic people and many organizations have one or two of them lying around. If you can fix them, do it. If you cannot fix them, remove them. If you cannot do either for one reason or another, it is important that you understand how to deal with toxic people. It is wise to resolve conflict by dealing directly with people who cause problems, but there will be scenarios where conflict resolution techniques do not work and/or problem solving may be out of your hands.

When a toxic person can no longer control you, they will attempt to control how other people think and feel about you. They will resort to spreading misinformation and try to damage your credibility. If you find yourself being dragged down by a toxic person, stay out of the mud. Do not let them bring you down to their level. When you are doing the right thing, only the wrong people will question it.

When firefighters approach a hazardous materials incident and are gathering information about what they are confronted with, they often implement Time, Distance, and Shielding measures (T-D-S) to minimize their exposure:

Time: Decreasing the amount of time spent near the source will decrease exposure.

Distance. Increasing distance from the source will decrease exposure.

Shielding. Increasing the shielding between you and the source will decrease exposure.

That is the same way you can deal with toxic people. If you cannot solve the problem for one reason or another, isolate the problem so it does not have a negative impact on you or the rest of your team.

Locate, Confine, and Extinguish Problems

Another popular phrase in the fire service lexicon describes the job of the suppression crew that is advancing a charged hose line into a structure. Their job is to Locate, Confine, and Extinguish the fire. This is the same thing you should do when it comes to problems and challenges. Your job is to locate the root of the problem, confine it, and extinguish it so it does not expand beyond its area or origin and cause additional problems.

Consider a fire in the growth stage. If it is not extinguished, it will continue to grow. The same thing can be said about problems in the workplace. That problem may be conflict among workers, an unacceptable performance, a bad attitude, or any other destructive behavior that can have a negative impact on your team. The solution is to stop that behavior from spreading, which may call for the implementation of conflict resolution techniques. My previous books (*Step Up and Lead* and *Step Up Your Teamwork*) have provided insight into conflict resolution, but it is worth repeating that passion is at the core of conflict. When two people are passionate about their opposing point of views, it is not uncommon for them to have a strained working relationship. One way around this is to understand that it is okay to disagree with someone, but it is not okay to disrespect them.

There are three ways that people typically deal with conflict. They ignore it, fight it out, or compromise. Ignoring it does not work because the problem will not simply disappear. It usually continues to increase, spread, or resurface in places where it should not. For example, two players arguing in the locker room is one thing, but those same two players carrying that argument onto the field or court during a game is another thing altogether. Do not ignore a sign of trouble when you see it, address it, so you can resolve it and minimize the damage. Fighting it out also does not solve the problem. When you fight it out, there will end up being a clear winner and a clear loser. This may work in times of war where the freedom of your country or community is at stake, but it rarely works in the workplace. The third option is the better of the three – compromise. To do so does not mean that you are compromising your integrity. Compromising is the process in which two parties try to determine a way in which they can both be satisfied with the outcome.

Compromising is a good thing, but do not compromise just to avoid confrontation. When it is time to draw the line and put your foot down, you must be ready, willing, and able to do just that. Conflict resolution requires courageous communication. Courage and confrontation go hand in hand. Confrontation is a difficult thing, but as the leader of a team or organization, you must have the courage to confront someone when they need to be confronted. This takes a willingness to be unpopular. To be clear, we are not talking about physical confrontation. We are talking about the confrontation that involves dialog, discussion, and debate, so you and your team can solve problems.

> Consider a fire in the growth stage. If it is not extinguished, it will continue to grow. The same thing can be said about problems in the workplace.

Do not back away from a debate. Healthy dialog, discussions, and debates about strategy and direction are necessary. Courageous communication means you are willing to allow all voices to be heard, and you are willing to have the difficult conversations that are often necessary to lead teams during challenging times.

Once you identify your problems, give your power and energy to the solutions. Meet with your team and talk about the solutions, then implement them. Consider ending important conversations with a method used by Kevin Plank, the founder of Under Armour. Plank concludes every meeting with a technique that helps him summarize what had occurred during the meeting. He recaps the following three things; what he heard, what he thinks, and what the team is going to do.

- This is what I heard,
- This is what I think, and
- This is what we are going to do.

Consider using that or a similar approach as a way of making sure the voices of those around you have been heard. Ask yourself:

- Did I hear them correctly?
- Did I express my opinion on the matter?
- Did I clearly explain our action plan moving forward?

Everyone must have a voice, and everyone deserved clarity because that is what is needed to enable a team to improve their performance.

Always solve problems before they escalate. If you are dealing with a large team of people who are working from remote areas, you may have no choice but to address issues in an email or through some other form of written communication. If that is your only option, do it. Otherwise, sending out an email or text is not the best way to mitigate problems. The better way is for people to see your face and hear your voice. That is how trust is earned.

Think of yourself as a problem solver and talk with the members of your team about them being problem solvers as well. If you do end up parting ways with a team member, do it without burning bridges. Part ways as amicably as you can and wish them luck because your paths are likely to cross again. After being cut from the 1960 Olympic Hockey Team, Herb Brooks called his father. In the book *Miracle in Lake Placid*, Brooks recalled that his father told him, "Keep your mouth shut, thank the coach, wish the players luck, and come home."

Herb Brooks would later become the coach of the 1980 men's Olympic hockey team that pulled off one of the greatest sports achievements in Olympic history. That story, which is told in the book and the movie *Miracle*, is another great example of having the guts to persist, as well as the fact that at some point in a fight, technique gives way to heart and determination.

> Right is right and wrong is wrong.
> Never let anyone convince you otherwise.

Embrace Discomfort

Comfort is a good thing. If you have good health, financial security, and peace of mind, that is a good thing. When you are trying to grow and improve, however, comfort is the enemy. In that aspect, comfort is overrated. Comfort does not necessary lead to happiness. In fact, comfort often makes people lazy and leads to discontent.

Discomfort is a catalyst for growth. Therefore, you must learn to get comfortable with being uncomfortable. If you struggle with this concept, here are four tips on how to embrace discomfort.

1. Get in the Game.

The first thing you will need to do is show up. Once you enter the arena and come face-to-face with the challenge in front of you, you may find that you were stressing out over something that is not as big of a deal as you originally thought it would be. If you ever competed in youth sports, you are probably familiar with those butterflies you felt before competition. You are also probably familiar with how those same butterflies seemed to disappear once the game began.

You may not win the battle just because you arrived, but you will have a 50/50 chance (or better if you prepared properly) because you are now in the game. If after you show up you are tempted to quit, good. Many successful people have wanted to quit most of the things that had eventually brought value and rewards to their lives. Whenever you begin something new, there is always a possibility that you will reach a point when you want to throw in the towel. When that happens, remind yourself that you have already made the commitment and you are going to see it through one way or another. The top producers in every field are completely committed to doing what it takes to thrive in their industry. They believe in themselves; they believe in their companies; they believe in their products and services; they believe in their customers, and they are committed to seeing the realization of their goals and dreams.

2.   Do Not Give Up.

Success and heroism often come down to pushing forward ten seconds longer than your opposition. Most people do not give up because something is hard. They give up because they do not see the finish line. They start to tell themselves that whatever they are trying to accomplish will take too long, but they fail to remind themselves that the time will pass anyway, so why not make the most of it by pushing forward. They may think it will be too hard, but they fail to realize that not seeing things through can be much more difficult and bring on unwanted hardship in the long run.

Persist until something great happens. Some say you cannot measure heart and determination, but history books tell a different story. History was shaped by people who refused to give up. If, however, it is true that you cannot measure heart and determination, I hope that one day you will be known for what could not be measured.

3.   Build Your Tribe.

One of the greatest ways to overcome your challenges is to surround yourself with like-minded people. Group support is a powerful thing. Holding each other accountable is critical. The fire service uses accountability systems for a reason – they work.

Teams of like-minded people offer strength and support. This is particularly true in the emergency services and the military. These men and women spend a large percentage of their daily life surrounded by the same people. They laugh together, cry together, eat three meals a day together, and experience horrific incidents together. Because of this, they share a special bond and have a strong support system. If you do not have this bond with others at work or in your personal life, try to create it.

Finding a tribe both at work and outside of work is imperative in dealing with the demons that haunt you. Humans are innately tribal, and they find solace – and strength – in groups of their peers.

4.   Stay Calm

When facing adversity, train yourself to be the calmest person in the room. Nothing is worse for an interior firefighting crew than hearing people outside of the structure screaming on the radio. The same can be said about the team manager in the board room, or head coach on the sidelines. Stay calm. If you are calm when there is chaos around you, people will see you as the one who is in control, and this will make your team feel confident.

Remaining calm in the face of adversity takes practice. This is a by-product of the type of training that has been described earlier in this book. A calm mind brings inner strength and self-confidence, and enables you to make rational, well-thought-out decisions.

Best-selling self-help author Wayne W. Dyer said, "Being relaxed, at peace with yourself, confident, emotionally neutral, loose, and free-floating – these are the keys to successful performance in almost everything."

> **Discomfort is a catalyst for growth.**

What do you see when you walk through a cemetery? You may be tempted to answer, tombstones. Beneath many of those tombstones, however, may be people who have died with their dreams unrealized. Maybe it was because they were unable or unwilling to get uncomfortable. Surely, they may have still lived good lives and shared many laughs with loved ones, but one cannot help but to walk through a cemetery and think about all the books that were never written, songs that were never sung, and businesses that were never developed. Do not let that happen to you. You only have so much time on this Earth, and you do not want to live with your talents untapped and your dreams unrealized. Embrace discomfort today, so you can begin to live the life you desire.

Chapter Recap
combustible tips to ignite your team

Many people have not run far enough on their first wind to discover that they had a second wind waiting in reserve. When you define your dream and begin moving toward it, you will inevitably encounter challenges. This is not likely; it is virtually "guaranteed." Embrace the struggle and the discomfort that comes with adversity, because the people who find a way to navigate their way through those challenges are the ones who end up reaching their destination – the prize.

Do not ever lose your will to fight. Those who do are often controlled by those who still have fight inside of them. You may be just one more call, one more swing, one small victory, one more interview, or one more try away from the success you desire, so keep moving forward. The difference between a master and a beginner is the master has failed more times than the beginner has even tried.

If you are struggling with things that have occurred in your past, that is understandable. You may have had to go through challenges that many others have not had to. Do not be deterred by your past. Instead, celebrate your past – failures included – no matter how difficult it may have been. Your past has given you the strength and wisdom you have today. Use that experience to your advantage. Be easy on yourself for mistakes you made in the past. You didn't know back then what you know now.

When you are tired, beat up, and feel like quitting, reach deep inside of yourself, and find a way to continue fighting and persist. You may be exhausted, but there comes a time in every fight where technique gives way to heart and determination.

6

ADAPT WHEN NECESSARY

*You must have a contingency plan for adversity
because you will encounter some.*

There are many reasons why a team may need to adapt. Among those reasons are poor planning, a failing strategy, or a rapidly changing environment. Those who serve in the emergency services know this well. Many years ago, a person became a firefighter and did just that… fought fires. Today, a firefighter understands they do much more than put the wet stuff on the hot stuff. It does not take long for the modern day firefighter to recognize that the job description has expanded to emergency medical technician, hazardous material first responder, extrication specialist, technical rescue expert, and a weapons-of-mass-destruction first responder who is positioned on the forefront of America's fight against terrorism. This is all in addition to the plumbing, electrician, and building construction knowledge they must have. Not to mention carbon monoxide and fire investigation knowledge.

In 2020, just when firefighters may have thought they had it all figured out, along came COVID-19 (aka coronavirus), which many immediately began referring to as "the new normal." The pandemic of 2020 was not the first "new normal" that firefighters had encountered. In the 1970s, EMS was the new normal. In the 1980s it was hazardous materials. In the 1990s it was urban search and rescue (USAR), which included high angle rescue and confined space operations. In 2000, they began navigating our way through white powder substances, followed by active shooter incidents and other acts of violence in 2010. 2020 started with a bang with the COVID-19 pandemic. What will the future bring? No one knows for sure, but one thing is for certain. Teams that succeed will have to find a way to adapt and overcome the next "new normal."

The global pandemic (COVID-19) initially hit my area in New Jersey hard in the first quarter of 2020. At first, many downplayed the virus and posted comments about how the Flu was more serious than this thing they were calling the coronavirus. Most people did not think it was going to be anything significant; however, their thought process began to change when officials began canceling or postponing all sporting events from recreation programs to professional sports. Even the Summer Olympic games of 2020 were rescheduled for 2021.

After halting sporting events, local government officials began urging people to stay home and stay isolated for at least two weeks if they believed that they made any type of contact with someone who was infected with COVID-19. In my state, that recommendation was quickly adapted by New Jersey Governor Phil Murphy who signed Executive Order No. 107, directing all state residents to stay at home until further notice. The order provided for certain exceptions, such as obtaining essential goods or services, seeking medical attention, visiting family, reporting to work, or engaging in outdoor activities.

In effort to strengthen the social distancing measures that were put in place, the order also prohibited all gatherings of individuals, such as parties, celebrations, or other social events. When in public, individuals were required to practice social distancing and stay at least six feet apart whenever possible, excluding immediate family members, caretakers, household members, or romantic partners.

Many states followed suit with similar Executive Orders, which directed the closure of all nonessential retail businesses to the public, with the exceptions of Grocery stores, farmers markets, farms that sold directly to customers, and other food stores; Pharmacies and medical marijuana dispensaries; Medical supply stores; Gas stations; Convenience stores; Ancillary stores within healthcare facilities; Hardware and home improvement stores; Banks and other financial institutions; Laundromats and dry-cleaning services; Stores that principally sold supplies for children under five years; Pet stores; Liquor stores; Car dealerships, but only for auto maintenance and repair, and auto mechanics; Printing and office supply shops; and Mail and delivery stores.

Many nonessential companies were granting temporary leaves of absence by letting go a portion of their work staff. Two weeks turned into one month, one month turned into two, then three. Some of the businesses that "temporarily" closed were unable to recover from the economic challenge and had to close their doors permanently.

During this time, Americans were introduced to terms and words that many of them had never heard before. Terms like social distancing, flattening the curve, remote learning, self-quarantine, contact tracing, community spread, and herd immunity.

As always, healthcare workers, law enforcement officers, and firefighters were among the essential employees who continued to answer the calls of people in distress, but they all needed to adapt the way they provided their services. All fire service organizations and agencies were affected in some way during the pandemic. Many lessons were learned with regards to communication, directives, deployment, infection control, purchasing, and legal and ethical decision making.

In his article "COVID-19: Rising Above the Fog of Unprecedented Change" (April 10, 2020; Firehouse.com), Deputy (Assistant) Chief Jacob McAfee of the North Central Fire District in California wrote about the astounding amount of change that occurred in our world and the fire service profession in just three months. McAfee referred to the pandemic as the ultimate VUCA environment (Volatile, Uncertain, Complex, and Ambiguous), which seemed to describe the new minute-by-minute reality of the tradition-rooted fire service perfectly.

During this time, decisions needed to be made quickly by people in leadership positions who were rapidly receiving new information. Firefighters were forced to adjust and make procedural changes daily. Communication with other organizations began happening through teleconferences, videos, and web-based meeting platforms. Leaders had to leave their egos at the door and seek advice from experts and other agencies they normally did not communicate with prior to the outbreak of the pandemic – a process called boundary spanning, which can be described as linking an organizations internal network with external sources of information.

In his article, McAfee brought attention to the fact that studying war while sitting behind a desk is a completely different thing than experiencing war from the trenches. He brought light to the fact that leadership roles can sometimes shield a person from the real hands-on work during times of great change, resulting in the loss of appreciation for those who are out there implementing the ideas and policies that they are being developed by office staff members.

> Studying war while sitting behind a desk is a completely different thing than experiencing war from the trenches.

In times of change, establishing trust is vitally important. The organizations that functioned successfully during the early stages of the pandemic were ones whose leadership were transparent with the rank and file. They were learning minute-by-minute and passing on information as they received it. Effective communication between all parties was equally as important because without it leaders simply could not be in touch with the emotional and mental state of their team members.

Many fire departments, which also provide EMS (first responder and/or paramedic services) for their community, began implementing a scout model for medical calls. They would send in one member suited up like a doctor, wearing latex gloves and an N95 surgical mask. That individual would gather information and assess the patient and situation, then make the decision based on the patient's signs and symptoms as to whether other members should enter and, if so, which equipment they should bring in with them.

The idea behind the scout model is a simple one, but at the same time incredibly complicated. The scout has one shot to get this right, with no room for error. If the scout makes the wrong decision, the entire crew can be exposed and therefore may become infected. This is a particularly challenging position for one individual to be in, especially since an infected person could be contagious yet asymptomatic and therefore not exhibit any signs or symptoms at all.

Each time patient contact was made, gloves had to be disposed of, and everything that could be disinfected needed to be. In addition, many of those who became infected were in the pre-symptomatic phase and did not exhibit any symptoms until after at least one week. Because of this, many first responders were sleeping in their vehicle or setting tents up in their garages for fear of exposing their family members and loved ones back home.

The pressure on this individual – the scout – was immense.

In one instance, navigating their way through this challenge was no different than any other because firefighters still had each other to rely upon and bounce ideas off; however, in another instance, this was completely new and uncharted waters. The fire service profession had always relied greatly on teamwork and peer support. At a working structure fire, for example, all hands were on the scene and working. If the department was lucky enough, there would be two, three, or more individuals at the command post making decisions based on the evolving situation. However, with a fire, they can see the enemy. With a virus, they cannot.

Many people were feeling the pressure of having to making important decisions at all levels. I had many conversations with firefighter, company officers, and chief officers who were all feeling the pressure and anxiety that comes with uncertainty and fear of the unknown. Firefighters, however, adapt. It is what they do. It is what they have always done and will continue to do. I spoke with one fire chief from northern New Jersey who was heading up an organization of roughly ninety-three members and when I asked him how things were going, his reply made me proud and confident, and described the firefighter mentality perfectly.

"I'm not going to lie. It has been rough, but I am very happy to be part of this organization during this time. Adversity exposes our weaknesses. I'm going to use what I learn here to help make our team stronger."

Chief Lou Venezia from the Bloomfield fire department impressed me with his reply that day, but I am not surprised. Having known Chief Venezia for the most of my adult life, I knew he was a person who had been through his share of adversity in his lifetime, and he had always used it to identify flaws, adapt, and make himself, and everyone around him, stronger.

> ## "Adversity exposes our weaknesses."
> ## —Chief Lou Venezia

The Training Officer

After seven years with my fire department, I had reached the rank of captain and was chosen to be the head of our training division. This was the result of a careful and thorough selection process on behalf of my organization. That process went something like this—no one else wanted to do it. I received the job by default; I was the junior guy. I remember our administrative deputy chief walking up to me and asking if I would be interested in taking the daytime position (which, by the way, was significantly more work than the line officer role that I was currently assigned to, and offered no additional financial compensation). My exact reply was, "What does the position entail?" After a brief conversation I told the deputy that I did not think it was the right position for me. It did not have anything to do with the financial aspect. I simply did not think I had the skillset needed for the job and quite frankly, I did not like the hours. A steady day job in administration was not as appealing as being a line offer on shift.

Apparently, that one innocent question, followed by a thirty-second conversation was all it took to seal my fate. Two days later, the chief of our department informed me that I was selected to be our organization's training officer. When I asked why he chose me, he said that I was the one who showed the most interest. Needless to say, I was not very happy. I remember talking with my brother, who was also a captain at the time, and expressing my concern.

"You're in a position where you can make great changes for our organization," he said.

"Changes? What kind of changes could I possibly make?" I said.

"What do you think we need?" he asked.

We talked about how all four groups operated differently and that we did not have any standard operating guidelines.

"Why don't you write them?" he asked and suggested at the same time.

"I don't know how to write an SOG," I replied.

"It's easy. You go to the Phoenix Fire Department's website, print theirs out, put our name on top, and you just wrote one," he answered in a half joking, half serious manner.

"If it's that easy, how come nobody has done it yet?" I rebutted.

"I don't know," he replied, "but they are not you."

My brother always gave me credit for being someone who stepped up to a challenge and did what needed to be done. A couple days after our conversation, we took a ride to Jersey City Fire Department headquarters, which was our neighboring department. After meeting with their training officer, I was able to obtain a copy of five of their Standard Operating Procedures, which enabled me to have a better understanding of SOP's and SOG's.

Instead of looking at my new position as an inconvenience, I quickly embraced the challenge and looked at it as an opportunity to improve my organization, as well as myself. Within a few years, I had developed a comprehensive set of standard operating guidelines, a probationary firefighter training program, and a variety of other training-related documents that my department will hopefully use for years to come. I also rose to the rank of deputy chief and wrote several books on tactics, leadership, team development, and customer service. I do not mention any of that to try to impress you, but rather to impress upon you that it was all a by-product of a position I did not want or think I would be good at.

Maybe you are currently working as your organization's training officer. You might even be called upon to become a grant writer, as I was. I did not even know if I had the ability to write the way a grant writer does. It was yet another challenge, but I accepted. Five years later, I had secured more than three million dollars in grant money for our organization. How does a person who takes a job as a firefighter end up adding grant writer to his job description? The answer is simple: in life and business, we must learn to adapt.

You already adapt. You have been doing so your entire life, but is it by choice? In other words, do you adapt because you have no other option, or because you are a leader who is looking for the one best way to accomplish a specific task? Being adaptable means that you are capable of quickly adjusting to rapidly changing conditions. This trait is paramount for all firefighters because situations escalate quickly on the fireground. It has been said a thousand times, but the fact is there are only two ways to put out a fire—out-resource it or out-think it. In today's fire service, it is becoming increasingly difficult to out-resource a fire. You must be able to out-think it, which requires the ability to adapt. Corporate America needs to take this page out of the fire service playbook. Your ability to evaluate and revise your strategy on the fly is imperative to your overall success.

> Your ability to evaluate and revise your strategy on the fly is imperative to your overall success.

To be adaptable, you must also be resourceful; meaning you are capable of skillfully, safely, and promptly navigating your way through a variety of situations, regardless of the tools, staffing, and resources that are—or are not—available at any given moment. If you are resourceful, you are creative, and you will always be looked at by others as a person with ingenuity, who shows initiative and can get the job done, no matter what.

Do not ever lose sight of the fact that the only time you grow is when you step outside of your comfort zone. You may be confident in one area of business, such as dealing with an unhappy customer. You may also handle pressure well, but what happened when you suddenly find yourself having to take on an administrative task that scares the heck out of you. Do not shy away from that challenge. Instead, tackle that task with vigor. Even if it makes you slightly uncomfortable. The truth is that we should never feel too comfortable in our job. In the fire service we have the mindset that the person who feels comfortable enough in his or her career to sit back, relax and think he or she is done learning is a danger to everyone. That holds true for any organization and team that wants to achieve success and remain at the top of their game.

Win The Position

Anyone who has ever competed in amateur wrestling at the high school or college level is aware that wrestling is a sport of constant movement, requiring a high level of physical exertion. Those who have a greater understanding of the sport; however, realize that it is more than just movement. Collegiate coaches, for example, want their wrestlers to understand that their goal is to win each position.

If you were to break down a seven-minute match that ended in a score of 5–4, it is obvious that the wrestler with the 5 points won the match, but before that individual won the match, he or she had to win a position, or two, or three, which resulted in a 1-point advantage. The score of the match, however, does not always tell the story of the match. It is not unheard of for a wrestler who was down by 4 points with less than thirty seconds left to pull off a 5-point move and end up with the win. A wrestler must always wrestle to win every position. If your opponent takes you down and scores two points, you may have lost that position, but now you are in a new position where you must adapt to your new situation and work to win that position. "Win the position" is the mindset that a wrestler should keep until the match is over, and that is also the mindset you should keep until the end of your game is finalized.

This principle works in every sport. In baseball, both the pitcher and batter have the goal to win each pitch, and both teams have the goal to win each inning. In football, the goal is to win each down, then series, then quarter, then half, and so on. If you lose a position, adjust. The end of a failed strategy is the beginning of a new strategy. This type of thought process brings us right back to Lt. General Hal Moore's second principles for leaders conduct in battle; There is always one more thing you can do to influence the situation in your favor, and after that one more thing, and after that one more thing, etc. etc.

> ## The end of a failed strategy is the beginning of a new strategy.

You will occasionally find yourself in what you believe to be a losing situation, but perhaps you just lost a last position, or two. The idea behind this concept is to adapt from what happened yesterday and focus on what you can to do win today. Yesterday is over and there is nothing you can do to get it back. You either already won or lost that day. If you won, build on it. If you lost, learn from it, grow, and go win today.

You Win or Your Learn

In 1968, the New York Jets football team was in its ninth season as a franchise in the National Football League. In the first few games of the season, fourth-year quarterback Joe Namath threw twelve interceptions. Namath, a University of Alabama alumni, quickly realized the goal was to win football games, not throw for 400 yards per game. He adapted and changed his play calling to favor a ground game and shorter passes.

The team finished the season with an 11–3 record and won the AFL Eastern Division before defeating the defending champion Oakland Raiders in the AFL championship game and advancing to Super Bowl III. The opposing Baltimore Colts, led by sixth-year head coach Don Shula and three-time league MVP quarterback Johnny Unitas, finished the regular season with a record of 13–1, and were the heavy favorites going into their game against the Jets.

Although they were the underdogs, "Broadway Joe" Namath famously guaranteed a victory. The Jets were leading the game in the fourth quarter when Coach Weeb Eubank asked Namath to throw a pass. Namath said he would rather run out the clock because the Colts could not score on defense. He did not throw one pass in the fourth quarter, and the Jets defeated the Colts 16–7 in a stunning upset.

In the locker room after the game, one reporter approached Namath and made a reference to Broadway Joe being "king of the hill."

The quarterback quickly shut that down and replied with, "No. We're king of the hill. We got the team, brother."

Namath showed that he had the ability to adapt. First, by transitioning to a ground game and shorter passes during the regular season; then by taking advantage of the strength of his team's running game during the Super Bowl. He also knew the goal was to win each down, then series, then quarter, then half, and continue until the final whistle was blown.

Sometimes you can do everything right and still fall short. I was coaching a travel baseball team one year that was on the verge of an undefeated season. Our boys were ranked number 1 in the division and were playing in a game against the number 3 seed. We knew they were going to be a tough team, but after four innings our team was winning 7–0. Our boys were hitting well, and our pitcher was on fire. After the 4th inning, I made the decision to take my pitcher out because he had thrown 68 pitches. The league minimum was 75, and we had two other experienced pitchers on standby, so it felt like the right decision. Our relief pitcher entered in the top of the 5th inning and went 3 up, 3 down. It always feels great when you make the right decision, and again, I felt I had done just that. The boys entered the 6th and final inning still in command with a 7–0 lead. Our offense loaded the bases but failed to score as we entered the bottom of the 6th, still with a seven-run lead. I sent our relief pitcher in again to close the game out, but this time he could not find the strike zone. He hit one player and walked three. I took a trip to the mound to talk with him and settle him down. He seemed fine, but he walked the next batter as well, bringing the score to 7–2 with no outs and the bases loaded. No worries, we had our closer in the bull pen warming up. This kid throws hard – real hard – and had more experience than all the other pitchers in our division. The challenge is that he is not always on, but when he is… watch out. He is practically unhittable. Lucky for us, he was on. Unfortunately, so was the other team. Every player that stepped into the batter box swung the bat with bad intentions and every single one of them made contact. Our team had the best defense in the league, so that was not the problem. The problem was that every ball found a hole and made its way past our infield. We ended up losing 8–7.

A coach will never forget the feeling of watching a 7–0 lead disappear in final inning. However, the reason why I chose to coach in the first place was to provide the young boys and girls on my teams with valuable life lessons that they can refer to in the future to help them navigate their way through life's hurdles. Every player on the field learned a lesson that day. Our players learned to never let your guard down or take a lead for granted. The other team learned you are never out of the fight unless you stop swinging the bat. As a coach, I learned that even when I think I am making all the correct decisions, we can still walk away with a loss.

This is not a new revelation for anyone, especially someone in the emergency services industry. Every firefighter knows there is no such thing as "undefeated" in the fire service.

I had taken command at many fires as a deputy chief, and many of them were your standard – show up, get to work, knock it down, and pack up – types of jobs. However, like most other chief officers, I have had my share of challenging jobs as well. I can recall several fires where multiple things went wrong. I have never had a "perfect job" in my career. I remember one young deputy chief once saying that all he wanted was a simple room-and-contents fire where he could hone his skills and fine-tune a few things with his team. I told him that he can have that fire every day by simulating it during training with his team.

Firefighters will walk away from some jobs feeling like they knocked it out of the park, and they will walk away from others feeling like they were just knocked out. Again, there is no such thing as "undefeated" in the fire service. There are also no perfect records in entrepreneurship. In fact, every successful entrepreneur that you know probably failed way more than they have succeeded, but they adapted along the way until they figured it out.

Too many people dwell on their losses. Let's face it – losing hurts. It sucks. However, if the setback you encounter is not a deathblow to your team, get over it. At the time this book was written, there were twelve champions in each of the twelve weight classes of the Ultimate Fighting Championship, and only one was undefeated. The best fighters in the world have lost fights. You will also lose a fight, but you must be willing to learn from it, get back up and fight again. This is not only essential for your success it is essential for your happiness. People feel the most accomplished when they are making progress. The secret to happiness is progress, and you cannot make progress without the ability to adapt.

> The secret to happiness is progress, and you cannot make progress without the ability to adapt.

When you make a mistake, own up to it, learn from it, and let go of it. It is okay to let go of what is gone so long as you keep the lesson. Mistakes are not meant to be repeated. If an individual or team continues to make the same mistake even though they know it produces a poor outcome, it can no longer be considered a mistake, it has become a conscious choice. Do not waste your time making excuses. You can make progress, or you can make excuses, but you cannot make both simultaneously.

Comfort Restricts Growth

Self-education is important for every profession and the fire service is no different. In fact, in our profession, self-education is significantly more important than in most others. Why? Because reading books, attending conferences, and watching industry related videos from professionals in the fire service is one of the ways we enhance our situational awareness and develop our instincts. Self-education is also one the best ways to keep yourself motivated.

One day, I reviewed my personal training records and realized I had more than 150 certificates for industry related seminars I attended over a fifteen-year period. It was not unusual for me to see many familiar faces at the same seminars during that time. I also do not think it is a coincidence that most of those people also became high ranking officers within their organizations. Make no mistake about it, there is a direct correlation between education and career advancement.

Early on in my career I remember hearing a speaker tell the audience, "The reason you attend a seminar is to hear the sentence, or two, that you needed to hear at that point in your life in order to help you obtain better results." As a student, I still attend seminars with that thought in mind. As a professional speaker, it has always been my goal to be the one who provides those words of wisdom for the people in attendance. I am sure you have heard a speaker say something like, "If I can get through to one person my time was worth it." I absolutely respect that goal, but it has never been mine. My intention has never been to reach one. My intention has always been to find a way to get through to everyone who has given me the gift of their time and attended my seminars. Whether it be through a story, a principle, or a single sentence, my specific intent has always been to say something that each person needed to hear on that day.

It was 0730 hours, and we were just coming to the end of one of our busiest twenty-four-hour shifts of the year. I was in my office reviewing some last-minute reports when my cell phone rang. I did not recognize the number, but I answered before realizing that my better option might have been to wait until I was driving home thirty minutes later to call the number back so I could focus on the reason for the call.

"Hello. This is Deputy Chief Viscuso," I said.

"Chief Viscuso. This is Chief Thomas from Massachusetts. I attended your leadership training at FCAM a couple months ago."

FCAM stands for Fire Chiefs Association of Massachusetts. Each year, FCAM hosts a professional development conference, and I had the honor of speaking at for the previous three years.

"Yes, Chief. How can I help you?"

"I just wanted to let you know that you have made a difference in my life and our organization."

"Really, how so?"

"Well, during your seminar you said the words, 'You cannot fix a problem if you refuse to acknowledge that it exists.' I normally do not take notes, but for some reason I wrote those words down. Over the next week, I kept thinking about those words. I felt like you were speaking directly to me."

Chief Thomas went on to say that shortly after the FCAM conference, he was complaining to a chief officer from another organization about a problem that he was having with a few of the members of his own organization.

He believed that when it came to department policies and organizational development, these specific members (two of whom were union officials) were selfish, stubborn, and unwilling to compromise. The union officials would often bypass Chief Thomas altogether and go directly to the Town Manager "behind his back" for answers. In return, the Town Manager would tell Chief Thomas what he wanted him to do, many times siding with the union instead of the chief.

"I thought it was me against the world," he explained, adding that he heard a rumor that the president of the Union was overheard saying that he was making it his personal goal to do whatever he could to get Chief Thomas fired.

As Chief Thomas explained the situation to his colleague, the other chief responded with some unexpectedly harsh words. "I hate to be the one to have to tell you this, but you are the problem," he stated bluntly.

"Me?" an agitated Chief Thomas replied. "What makes you think I am the problem?"

"The officers feel like they cannot communicate with you because you don't show them any respect, so they go over your head."

Chief Thomas relayed to me that he was initially agitated, but then he went on to share his revelation. Later that night he was contemplating what his colleague had said and wondering if it could be true. Then he remembered the words he heard at the seminar – You cannot fix a problem if you refuse to acknowledge that it exists – and it suddenly became clear to him that he was the problem, or at least part of it. This was a very uncomfortable revelation for the chief, who knew he was going to have to step away from his comfort zone if he intended to fix the problem.

On the next workday, he asked to meet with the union president and the other members he was having this issue with. They gathered in the conference room at work. Surely, they were wondering why Chief Thomas called for the meeting. None of them expected to hear what he was about to say.

"I wanted to bring you here today to apologize to you," he began. "I have misjudged you all, and wrongfully concluded that you were not interested in communicating or compromising. I have not shown you respect, and I now realize that the problem was me. I am the one who was not communicating properly. More to the point, I am the one who has not been listening to your ideas or concerns, and for that I am sorry. The conflict that has consumed our working relationship is a result of my failure to understand and respect all of you. I would like to start over and see what we can accomplish if we work together."

After a moment of stunned silence, the head of the union spoke up. "Chief, we realize we won't always get what we want, but all we really want is to be heard and understood."

Chief Thomas went on to explain to me that their working relationship has improved significantly since that conversation. "It was uncomfortable for me to come to that realization, but I decided to take this opportunity to show some humility. My failure to acknowledge their needs and look for a way to compromise was in some ways an act of stubbornness and cowardice. Chief Viscuso, you planted the seed. My colleague watered the ground. Your words and his blunt assessment were what I needed to hear to resolve my problem. Please share this story because I think it might help some other people."

> # You cannot fix a problem if you refuse to acknowledge that it exists.

The story you just read represents a common one that is often found in the workplace. It is a story about conflict and resolution. At the root of all conflict is a difference in belief systems. If I were born and raised in the city, for example, and you were born in the country, we would certainly have a different set of life experiences and upbringings. With those experiences we would both have already formed our beliefs. When two people meet and begin working together, there will come a time when they realize that they disagree on something (and sometimes on everything). Some people are so passionate about their point of view that they feel threatened by people who think differently. Don't lose sight of the fast that conflict is often a result of passion. A confident leader will want to be surrounded by passionate people. The key is to be respectful of the opposing point of view. If you can agree to disagree about things like politics and religion, and still stay focused on making a commitment to the overall mission, you can overcome conflict.

This story is a great way for us to revisit the three ways that most people deal with conflict – ignoring, fighting, or compromising. It cannot be expressed enough that at the core of conflict resolution is the word respect. If you disagree with someone, try to see things from their point of view.

Respect that person and try to understand why something may be important to him or her. You do not have to agree with them, you only need to understand that their opinion on the matter carries just as much weight with them as your opinion does with you. You can disagree with others without hating them.

When dealing with conflict, take your ego out of the equation. The best ideas must win, even when they are not your ideas. This can be a difficult concept for some people in leadership positions to grasp, however, it can be the exact thing your organization may need if you intend to achieve the performance outcome you desire.

Tom Landry, legendary coach of the Dallas Cowboy once said, "There's a misconception about teamwork. Teamwork is the ability to have different thoughts about things; it is the ability to argue and stand up and say loud and strong what you feel. But in the end, it's also the ability to adjust to what is the best for the team."

Learning From the Past

The United States Armed Forces use After Action Reviews (AAR) to help learn from past experiences and prepare for future ones. The AAR is a structured review or debriefing method for analyzing what happened, why it happened, and how things can be done better. The basic idea behind the AAR is to discuss what happened. The objective is to determine what the team was supposed to do and what the desired outcome was, and to compare that to what ended up happening. During the AAR it is important to talk about what you did well during the planning, preparation, and execution phases of the operation so you can talk about how to sustain the correct activity. Then follow that up by thoroughly discussing areas where the team can make improvements.

The formal AAR was originally developed by the U.S. Army. The concept works and has been adapted by many non-military organizations, both domestic and international. The fire service has also come to know the AAR by another term – the Post Incident Analysis (PIA), which we typically conduct after each significant incident. An AAR or PIA can be done by simply by asking these four questions:

1.   What was our overall mission?

2.   What did we do well?

3.   What could we have done better or differently?

4.   Who do we need to inform?

The fact that both the AAR and the PIA are remarkably similar is no coincidence. Many of the leadership and team development methods we use in the fire service are modeled after those that our military institutions have been using for years. If during an AAR you were to discover a problem with the technique, systems, or performance of your team, you must address the issue immediately. One way to do this is by assigning someone, or a team of people, to come up with a solution that can be used to correct the situation. If you do not take steps to fix the issue of concern, you are just admiring the problem. There needs to be an emphasis on "HOW" and "WHEN" you are going to fix the problem, and "WHO" is going to help you do it.

The focus on an AAR or PIA must remain on finding better ways to improve. If you are not discussing ways to improve, you are not leading a team. In fact, if you are not actively seeking better ways to prepare and improve, you are failing in the role as a team leader. Continuous improvement is what every high-performance organization should strive for.

> If you are not actively seeking better ways to prepare and improve, you are failing in the role as a team leader.

There are additional benefits that come with having AARs or PIAs with your team members. They also provide you with an opportunity to get together and discuss some other issues that may need attention around that time. I once scheduled a PIA after a structure fire where our members performed exceptionally well. Prior to starting the PIA, I introduced an issue that was on my mind.

"We need a motto," I said. "Microsoft is a brand, Coca-Cola is a brand, the United States Fire Administration is a brand, but what's our team's brand? They have mission statements and vision statements that express their core values. We need a motto that expresses our core values as well. Think about it and let me know if you have any ideas."

Before we finished discussing what we did right and what we could have done better, my cell phone vibrated. I glanced at my phone and saw that one of the firefighters in the room had sent me a text message. It read: Courtesy, Courage, and Commitment.

At that moment, our core values were identified and summed up in three simple words. Group C: Courtesy, Courage, and Commitment.

- Courtesy: consideration, cooperation, and generosity in providing service.

- Courage: mental or moral strength to venture, persevere, and withstand danger, fear, or difficulty.

- Commitment: an act of committing to a charge or trust, and in our case our community, organization, and each other.

We were a family, and being a family is not always easy. A family may care about each other, but sometimes they also have disagreements and fight amongst each other. When push comes to shove, however, a strong family will protect one another. We were a family built on Courtesy, Courage, and Commitment. If you intend for your team to perform at the highest possible level, you will have to become a family as well – a family that learns from the past but does not live in it.

AARs and PIAs provide great opportunities to bring your team together and strengthen that bond. Just remember that you win or lose as a team. In public service, business, and sports, when you are working as a team, do not ever blame one individual when you lose. There are many factors that contribute to winning, and the same can be said about losing. Look at the bigger picture. If a teammate is not performing to the best of his or her ability or if that induvial is in a slump, they already know they are struggling. You will need to address it but do so in private. They do not need to be blamed and shamed for the overall failure of the team in front of everyone.

When you need to adapt the mission, the strategy, or the message, some may need to tweak a couple minor things, while others may need to change significantly. You may need to have a difficult conversation with one or more of your team members, and that is okay. Just remind them that you are one team with one mission. You win together, you lose together, you adapt together, and you endure together.

Adapting the Mission and the Message

What is your mission and your message? That is a question that only you and your team can answer. It is also a question you should ask periodically because in a rapidly moving world, you will sometimes be in a situation where you must quickly change the way you are thinking, as well as the way you are doing things.

In chapter 1, we explored the question what is your mission? In that section we covered the three questions you should ask yourself, and your team regularly to help your team achieve better results.

Those questions are:

- What are we doing well that we need to KEEP doing?
- What are we doing wrong that we need to STOP doing?
- What aren't we doing that we need to START doing?

Refer to that section often as a reminder of how you can deliberately shape the culture of your organization by bringing your key players together and talking about what you should keep, stop, and start doing. Always involve the right people in making the decisions that affect training, procedures, and equipment.

You will come to realize that there will be times when the mission, or the message needs to adapt. Iconic investor Warren Buffet once said, "Should you find yourself in a chronically leaking boat, energy devoted to changing vessels is likely to be more productive than energy devoted to patching leaks." In other words, ditch the stubbornness and know when it is time to adapt your mission or your message.

> Always involve the right people in making the decisions that affect training, procedures, and equipment.

Review, Evaluate and Revise

When you encounter rapidly changing conditions it essential that you Review, Evaluate, and Revise your tactics regularly to ensure you are constantly meeting your goals. These three words are crucial in the fire service. Firefighters are constantly dealing with rapidly changing conditions on the fireground and must review, evaluate, and revise their tactics regularly to ensure they are constantly meeting their goals of life safety, incident stabilization, and property conservation. It does not matter if they are working at a hostile and intense fire scene or developing a pre-plan. Whatever the team is trying to accomplish, the R.E.R. concept will serve their team well.

This concept will serve any team well.

The principle behind R.E.R. is a simple one. If what you and your team are doing is working, keep doing it. If what you and your team are doing is not working, evaluate your actions and revise them, otherwise you will make the mistake many teams make and keep doing the wrong activity. If you are not achieving the results you want, you are either doing the wrong activity, or not enough of the right activity. Either way, you would have to review, evaluate, and revise your tactics so you can adapt and begin getting the results you want.

Teams that achieve the highest level of success are great at putting their heads together and figuring out what the best way to accomplish their goal is. The movie Apollo 13 has a great scene in it that illustrates this concept. In the scene, a group of engineers and scientists gather to come up with a plan to safely return three astronauts who are stranded on a space capsule. One of the scientists dumps a bunch of supplies on a table. They were the same items that the stranded crew on Apollo 13 had access to. He then says, "Okay, listen up. The people upstairs handed us this one and we gotta come through. We have to find a way to make this (he holds up a 1 ft x 1 ft square CO_2 scrubber) fit into the hole for this (he holds up a round tube-like filtration hole with smaller dimensions) using nothing but that (he points to the remaining items on the table)." Without hesitation, they begin shifting through the supplies to find a solution for making a square peg fit into a round hole.

Maybe the stakes are not as high as the ones in the movie, but your team may be confronted with those types of situations regularly. Meaning, the types of situations where you must concentrate on solving an urgent problem with a limited supply of available resources. To do this well, you must review, evaluate, and revise. You must adapt, which is a cornerstone of successful teamwork.

> ## Whatever you are not changing
> ## you are choosing.

When in doubt as to whether you should change something in your organization or leave it the way it is, consider the fact that whatever you are not changing, you are choosing.

Chapter Recap
combustible tips to ignite your team

American business magnate, investor, and philanthropist Warren Buffet said, "No successful person is mistake-free, and that's a good thing. Each stumble is a chance to learn and a warning when you're tempted to do something similar in the future." Adopt the philosophy that you are either going to win or you are going to learn. Learning requires the ability to adapt. Being adaptable means that you are capable of quickly adjusting to rapidly changing conditions. Your ability to evaluate and revise your strategies on the fly is imperative. An adaptable person is a benefit to any organization. They are resourceful and can skillfully, safely, and promptly navigate their way through a variety of situations, regardless of the available tools, staffing, and resources.

Change is inevitable, but many people fail to achieve success because they do not take corrective action soon enough. The first step to solving any problem is recognizing when there is one. Do not fall into the trap of thinking that you are the one who must always have the correct solution. You are human just like everyone else, and humans make mistakes. Educate yourself, learn from others, discuss your options with your team members and let the best ideas win.

One of the hardest decisions you will ever face in life is choosing whether to walk away or try harder. Walking away from a toxic environment that cannot be fixed, or a strategy that is causing more harm than good is part of the growing and learning process. When you weigh your options, take the path that makes the most sense for everyone involved. Do not fear change, it is often a very necessary part of life. When in doubt as to whether you should change something in your organization or leave it the way it is, it would be wise to remind yourself that whatever you are not changing, you are choosing.

The most important thing to remember is that once you adapt your strategy or tactics, you must go back and ensure that the rest of your team is in sync with you. If not, repeat steps 1 through 5 and remember, you must always have a contingency plan for adversity, because you are going to encounter some.

7

SERVE ALL AND SERVE WELL

*Always strive to exceed customer
expectations–not sometimes, always.*

I was once asked to speak about stress management to municipal workers from 11 counties at an annual leadership luncheon. During a conversation with the event organizer, I wanted more specifics, so I asked him to elaborate on what type of stress he was talking about.

"Not critical incident stress management. We would like you to talk about stress in the workplace. You know, the type of stress that comes from…" there was a lengthy pause.

I sensed that he was hesitant to say what he wanted to, so I thought I would help him out.

"Bad bosses?"

"Exactly," he confirmed.

A couple months later, I stood in front of a room of 120 administrative officers, clerks, and department heads to give a forty-five-minute presentation titled: "Stress Management: Preventing and Avoiding Mental and Physical Burnout." I began with a discussion on common sources of workplace stress. The list included the following:

- Low salaries
- Excessive workloads
- Lack of social support
- Work that is not engaging or challenging
- Inequality in responsibilities
- Few opportunities for growth or advancement

I asked if anyone in the room wanted to add anything to the list. One municipal government employee with thirty-five years on the books raised his hand. When I called on him, he quickly blurted out, "Poor leadership, organizational dysfunction, no positive feedback, lack of direction, drama, feeling underappreciated, and lack of fairness."

"Wow, did you rehearse that?" I asked.

Many of the other attendees laughed.

"No," he replied, "but I've lived it for thirty-five years."

I asked if any of the others in the audience felt the same way, and more than 90 percent of the attendees raised their hands.

Unfortunately, toxic cultures created by bad bosses or poor management are not uncommon in the workplace. This occurs everywhere, even in the fire service profession, which has often been referred to as the "greatest job on Earth." Earlier in this book, I mentioned that most polls in America rank firefighting among the top professions with regards to career satisfaction, which is why many in that profession find it interesting that in recent years there appears to be a growing number of firefighters who seem bitter, frustrated, and sometimes disgruntled to a point where they begin counting down the days to retirement many months, and sometimes years, before they are eligible.

I spoke with the members of one fire department that had an estimated 15 percent of their members – most of their veteran core – leave the job before they originally intended. One of the members told me that their team was consumed with drama. He said that many of his co-workers regularly made statements like, "I don't care anymore," and "I give up." He also made it a point to stress that, in his opinion, the brotherhood was dead. As I dug deeper into this with him, it became abundantly clear that his frustration had little to do with a "lack of brotherhood" and everything to do with poor leadership. This individual eventually admitted to me that he agreed firefighting was the greatest job on Earth, but at the same time, he was still counting down the days until he could leave what he described as a "toxic, soul-killing environment." During our group discussion, it became abundantly clear that most of the members of that organization loved the job, but they attributed their discontent to failed leadership and poor management.

> Unfortunately, toxic cultures created by bad bosses or poor management are not uncommon in the workplace.

Let that sink in for a moment. They love the job but want to leave it. My conversation with these firefighters reminded me that people leave managers, not companies. In fact, Gallup, Inc. (an American research-based, global

146

performance-management consulting company) reported that 75 percent of workers who voluntarily left their jobs did so because of their bosses and not the position itself.

Leaders who micro-manage or make their decisions based on fear, greed or ego often create a stressful working environment. Chances are, most people in leadership positions inherit a certain level of stress by the nature of their job as it is, so they certainly would not want any additional, unnecessary stress that comes from a bad supervisor. It is for that same reason that you do not want to be the individual who creates that stress throughout your team through faulty leadership on your part.

Unnecessary stress in the workplace in never a good thing. When we feel stress, our bodies release cortisol. Cortisol has been referred to as the "fight-or-flight" hormone. It lets you know when you are in danger; however, too much of it can impair rational thinking and decision making. If you work in a toxic culture, you are biologically more likely to make decisions that can lead to bad outcomes.

Do you want a bad outcome or a good one?

Yes, that was a stupid question; however, we see it all the time – a team of talented people being led by an individual who puts "ME" before "WE." If you worked for a person like that, good. I am glad you have had that experience, because you can learn just as much from a bad boss as you can from a good one. You can learn what not to do.

The Magic at Disney

If you have ever been to Disney Land or Disney World, you probably know they have a great reputation for providing exceptional service. If someone were to ask you what impresses you the most about Disney, you would probably use words like; clean, organized, friendly, magical, and great customer service. There is a reason why so many people answer this question using the same words. There is a reason why people always answer using the same words. Disney has systems in place to make sure they hold a high standard in these areas. For example, the park is always clean partly because it feels like there is a garbage can just about every sixty feet. There is always one in sight when you are looking to dispose of something. Another way Disney keeps their parks clean, is they do not sell chewing gum or peanuts. While cast members still must pry gum (brought in by guests) off the ground, tables, and other areas, not allowing guests to purchase more gum at their parks helps lighten the workload. Having a clean park, however, is not the key ingredient to Disney's reputation. Parks do not clean themselves. People clean them. You have likely been in 2,000-square-foot businesses that looked like they were just hit with a Category 5 hurricane. Disney World's land area exceeds 10,500 square miles, yet you would be hard pressed to find a candy wrapper on the ground.

If you want to have a better understanding as to how they achieve and maintain such a high standard, pick up some books written about Disney and begin researching. One book that I would recommend is *Creating Magic, 10 Common Sense Leadership Strategies from a Life at Disney*. *Creating Magic* was written by Lee Cockerell, the former executive VP of operations at Walt Disney World Resort. On page 5, Cockerell wrote the following:

What really drives the magic at Disney is the extraordinary service. How does Disney maintain that high quality of service? Each of the fifty-nine thousand Cast Members is trained to treat each and every guest with the utmost care and respect, and they do this consistently because they are treated exactly the same way by the Disney leadership; with the utmost care and respect.

That message is a powerful one that all organizational leadership can learn from. Take note of the words *care* and *respect*. The cast members are trained to treat the guests with care and respect, and Disney leadership treats the cast members with care and respect. Imagine living in a world where everyone treated each other with care and respect. Unfortunately, that will never happen, but it can and should happen on your team, and it all starts with you.

We all know that respect is not given, it is earned; however, there should also be a second part to that saying that we need to start acknowledging. Respect is not given, it is earned, but if you do not give it, you will not get it in return.

Eight Things to Avoid

Anyone who is familiar with my work knows that my main objective is to provide people, especially those in influential positions, with tools and ideas that will help them create a healthy working environment and strong culture. For that reason, most of the articles and books I have written have a positive message. In 2019, however, I had written an article titled "How to Kill Morale." The reason for this uncharacteristic style was simple. I want to remind everyone that dysfunctional leadership can kill the soul of an organization.

The surprising thing about this article is that it ended up going viral, mainly because many people seemed to be working for organizations that were doing one or more of the things listed in the article. The eight morale-killing actions mentioned were:

1. Do not play favorites.
2. Do not micro-manage
3. Do not have unnecessary/unproductive meeting
4. Do not give "busy work"
5. Do not hold grudges
6. Do not create a stressful working environment
7. Do not use discipline as a fear tactic
8. Do not disrespect your team members

Earlier in this chapter you read the sentence; *you can learn just as much from a bad boss as you can from a good one.* That is as true a statement as I have ever heard. Unfortunately, *bad leaders* do not know that they are bad, which is why it is so important for you to understand how your actions can negatively affect those under your charge. Do not do the eight things listed above unless your goal is to draw the minimum performance out of your team members and destroy the morale of your organization. If you are guilty of doing some of these things, do not be too hard on yourself. We are all guilty of doing the wrong things until we learned what the right things to do were. Learn from the past, but do not live there. It is time for you to step up and take charge. To paraphrase an old proverb, the best time to plant a tree is twenty-years ago. The second-best time is today. Do not dwell in the past and do not procrastinate any longer. Take corrective action today.

If you spend all your time looking for ways to punish your team or find reasons to hurt them instead of helping them improve, you are not a leader. You are simply occupying a leadership position within your organization. You may think you are surrounded by loyal people because they have become good at saying, "Yes Sir" or "Yes Ma'am," but it may be because they are scared to death that you are going to go after them. You may be leading by way of intimidation. If that is you, there will be a wonderful celebration when you retire, but you will not be invited to it because they are celebrating the fact that you are finally gone in a similar way that the rebels celebrated when the Sith Lord was killed in *Star Wars: the Rise of Skywalker.* (Sorry for that reference. I was looking for an appropriate analogy and I could not hold back my inner geek).

Do not misinterpret this message to read that you should never discipline your team members. When a person is doing the wrong activity, it must be corrected. For example, A fire chief will have to discipline his or her team members when they partake in unsafe, unethical, or rogue behavior. Sometimes the rank and file do not understand this, but a chief officer has been to places where the firefighters and first level officers have not yet been. Therefore, the higher-ranking officer would likely have a better understanding as to rules, regulations, policies, and acceptable practices. The point is to use discipline the correct way. Legendary UCLA men's basketball coach John Wooden said, "Discipline of others isn't punishment. You discipline to help, to improve, to correct, to prevent, not to punish, humiliate or retaliate."

> "You discipline to help, to improve, to correct, to prevent, not to punish, humiliate or retaliate." —John Wooden

When a person on your team is not doing the right activity, try to determine if the person is unaware, unable, or unwilling; then take the correct actions needed to resolve the issue.

The 3 Us are worth reviewing because they will help anybody determine what actions to take when an individual or team is not performing at the level they should be.

- Unaware

- Unable

- Unwilling

A person who is Unaware is not aware, or not conscious with regard to what is going on – meaning, they do not even know what they are doing is wrong. The action to take in that instance is to sit the person down and explain to them what they are doing incorrectly and what they need to do differently. Once they are aware, if they continue doing things incorrectly, they are now either Unable or Unwilling.

A person who is Unable, may not be capable of doing a specific task. For example, not every kid on a baseball team can be a pitcher or catcher. It would be foolish for a coach to get mad at a kid who cannot pitch if the first time he stood on the pitcher's mound was in the final inning of a championship game. Remember, everybody has talent, skills, and ability. Just because someone on your team is a poor performer in one area, does not mean they cannot be a strong contributor in another area. Find out what people are good at and assign them tasks accordingly. Also take into consideration that a person who is unable to do something today, may be capable of doing that thing tomorrow (or in the future) with the proper guidance and training, so don't be too quick to label a person as being unable to do a specific task.

The person who is unwilling is the one who presents the biggest challenge for an organization. An unwilling person is one who boldly resists authority and has a defiant attitude. In the military and fire service, these people are insubordinate, and insubordination results in serious consequences for the unwilling parties.

People in the emergency services typically get themselves in trouble in one of two areas. The first is when they are called to respond to high-risk, low-frequency incidents. These are heavy-consequence incidents they do not see often, and therefore require skills that they probably do not train on enough to ensure a successful outcome. Examples of high-risk incidents include confined space rescues for firefighters, or riots for law enforcement officials. High-risk, low-frequency incidents pose a threat to every organization, but they pose a much greater physical threat to emergency service workers, such as firefighters, law enforcement officers and of course our military.

Second place people get themselves in trouble is when they are unwilling to do the things they are supposed to be doing. In other words, they simply do not care to do the right activity. Barring extenuating circumstances like a traumatic incident that they may be having a difficult time working through, these people are usually the ones that need to be disciplined and possibly *let go* before they spread their defiant behavior throughout the team.

Your goal should be simple. Treat your team right and hold them to a high standard by ensuring that they treat the people that your organization serves with care and respect. If you are leading a team without showing respect to your team members, you are going to fail because they, in turn, are unlikely to show respect to each other or the people they serve. Disrespecting people in any scenario will never have a favorable outcome as illustrated in the following story about the angry traveler. As you read it, keep in mind that there is a right way and a wrong way to treat everyone. It is okay to disagree with people, but it is never okay to disrespect them.

> It is okay to disagree with people, but it is never okay to disrespect them.

Lost Luggage and the Angry Traveler

One of the true joys of my career as a speaker has been having the opportunity to travel throughout the world to work with amazing people and organizations. One year, my travels brought me to NSA Souda Bay in Crete, Greece, where I was invited by the fire chief to speak for three days. When an opportunity like that arises, you can imagine how exciting it is for both me and my wife because this is a dream location that enables us to mix business with pleasure. That said, the beginning of our trip did not exactly fall into the dream category.

As we waited in JFK airport in New York for the first of our two flights, the gate agent informed us that the flight was cancelled due to mechanical issues. We were advised to go to the counter to seek another flight that would get us to our destination. After looking at our options, we ended up having to take a different route that now required three flight segments to Crete instead of two. Our original flight was from JFK to London then from London to Crete, with a ninety-minute layover. The new itinerary was JFK to London, London to Athens, then Athens to Crete, with less than 30 minutes in between each flight segment. Although the agent told us we should have no problem making the flights, I travel enough that I anticipated the most likely challenge ahead.

"Put your bag next to mine," I said to my wife.

"Why?" she asked.

"We may make it onto all three flights, but in all probability, our bags will not," I answered.

"Are you serious?" she asked. "What are we going to do?"

"I wouldn't worry about it. They will eventually get our bags to us, but I sincerely doubt our bags are going to make it to Crete when we initially arrive," I explained.

I snapped a photo of the bags and told my wife that I would show it to the person in the lost baggage department if my prediction came true.

When we arrived in Crete after a long day of travel, it did not come as a surprise to either of us when our bags did not appear on the turntable. We watched as the other travelers reclaimed their luggage and left the airport. In the end, the only one's waiting were my wife and I, and two women in their late thirties. My wife began talking with one of them, whose eyes stayed locked on the opening in the wall where the luggage would enter the room. She was obviously still hoping they would appear – a long shot since the turn luggage conveyor had already stopped moving.

"Did you come from JFK also?" my wife asked.

"Yes," the woman replied. She was clearly disappointed.

As this conversation began, the other woman was pacing back and forth like an MMA fighter waiting for the referee to start the fight. This woman was beyond disappointed. She was outright furious, and she wanted to make sure everyone in the airport knew how she felt.

"This is B***-****!" she barked, before going into one of the most profanity filled rants that I have every heard in my life. Since I come from Northern, New Jersey, and a stone's throw away from Manhattan, that is saying a lot.

"You people S***!" she continued. "I knew this was going to happen. This is absolute B***-****!"

As this was happening, I walked up to one of the two young ladies that were working in the dreaded *lost baggage claim* department. I already felt sorry for them knowing that they were going to be berated by the other customer, but I blocked that out, and focused on the woman who was there to help me find my luggage.

"Hello, how are you?" I asked.

"I'm good, thank you," she replied in broken English, "Are you looking for your luggage?"

"We are," I said, as I lifted my phone and showed her the photo I took of our checked bags when we were at JFK.

"That's very helpful," she replied. The woman handed me a claim form, "Can you please fill this out for me. This form will help us locate your luggage."

As I filled out the form which included my contact information, flight details, and luggage type, I could not help but to hear the conversation that was happening between the angry traveler and the other woman who was working in the lost baggage claim department. The angry traveler was relentlessly yelling at the airport worker, barking profanities, and blaming this woman and everyone else for her troubles.

I completed the form and handed it to the woman who was helping me. She then proceeded to professionally tell me what the next steps would be.

"There is another flight departing from Athens at midnight tonight," she said. "I will try to make sure your luggage gets on that flight. If so, we will text your cell number to let you know we received it. No one will be available to take it to your hotel until the morning, but we will get it to you before nine o'clock."

"Thank you," I replied.

"You're welcome. If by chance you did not hear from us, call this number," she added, pointing to a number on the form. "When you call that number, this phone right here on the desk will ring. One of us will be here to pick it up. If no one answers, call this other number. This one is the direct number to your airline. If you give them your claim number, they will also be able to tell you where your luggage is."

"Fantastic," I said. "I appreciate your help."

As this was happening, the angry traveler was still swinging her arms and yelling at the other worker behind the counter. The thought crossed my mind that this must be why some Europeans dislike Americans. Finally, after getting fed up with the insults and attacks, the woman working behind the counter said, "I cannot help you."

"What!?" the angry traveler barked. "What do you mean you can't help me! You lost my bags and now you're telling me you can't help me!"

"I cannot help you," the woman repeated. "You will have to call your airline."

After one last barrage of insults, the angry traveler stormed off. I could not help but to wonder how she could be so blind with anger that she did not even realize I was being helped with the same challenge that she was having. The only difference was that I was not treating the one person who was helping me as if she'd caused the problem. On the contrary, the woman working in the lost baggage department was solely there to solve my problem.

Moments after the angry traveler left, the woman who was helping me circled another number on the paper and said, "I also wrote this number down for you. When you get back home, call this number. Since your flight was changed and delayed, and your bags were lost, they will compensate you for the inconvenience by refunding a portion of the money you spent on the tickets."

"Really? Thank you," I replied.

I can honestly tell you that I did not expect any compensation at all, but when I returned home to the United States, I called the number and followed their directions by filing a claim on their website. Three weeks later, the airline sent me a sizeable check that more than compensated us for our troubles.

It is obvious which one of us had the better experience. It should also be obvious why. As a person who writes and teaches about how to provide quality customer service, I do not condone the way the other worker treated the angry traveler. I would never accept that from someone on my team, but as a human being, I do understand why it happened. The angry traveler disrespected the airport worker and because of this, she received the same treatment in return. The story illustrates the point about respect from earlier in this chapter. Respect is not given, it is earned… but if you do not give it, you will not get it in return.

More Than Expected

There are three simple steps you will want to take when interacting with your community and customers. They are: (1) Smile, (2) Respect the customer, and (3) Exceed their expectations. To help you do this try to imagine that everyone you meet is wearing a sign that says, "Make me feel important."

I was running a little behind schedule one morning when I walked into a local coffee shop for the first time and ordered an everything bagel, toasted with cream cheese, and a hot tea with honey.

"Your name?" asked the middle-aged woman working behind the counter.

"Frank," I replied.

Moments later, the woman handed me my order.

"Is the honey already in the tea?" I asked.

"Yes," she replied, with a warm smile.

"Great, how many packets did you use?"

"One."

"Can I get two more please?"

"Of course," she answered, handing me two additional packets of honey.

As I was leaving, she wished me a nice day and thanked me for coming in.

On the following day I decided to stop at that same coffee shop because of the warm, friendly environment and comfortable vibe that I felt during my initial visit. I was surprised when I entered through the front door only to be greeted by the friendly woman with, "Hi, Frank. How are you today?"

I said, "Hi. I am great. How are you?"

"I am doing great also. Thank you for asking," she replied. "Would you like the usual?"

The usual, I thought. *There is no way she remembers my order. I was only here one time.* My initial thought was to repeat my order to make sure she knew what I wanted, but I was also curious what she thought my usual was, so I decided to play the game.

"Sure," I answered.

I made conversation with her as I watched her prepare one everything bagel, toasted with cream cheese, and a hot tea with three honey packets. I left that coffee shop knowing it would be the one I would be going to moving forward. How did that coffee shop earn my business? The bagel and tea tasted no different than it did at two other local places I frequented, but the friendly woman behind the counter at this coffee shop did something the employees at the other ones did not. She made me feel important.

> # Imagine that everyone you meet is wearing a sign that says: "Make me feel important."

She could have just taken my order and given me what I'd asked for. I would have been perfectly satisfied, but she understood that there were a dozen other places I could have gone to for a bagel and tea; if they wanted to earn a new customer's business on a regular basis, it would benefit them to do more than expected.

You want to have satisfied customers, but do not simply settle for that as your overall goal. If you think about it, having a satisfied customer is the lowest bar you can hit and still stay in business. If you owned a construction company and one of your clients was asked if they were happy with the results your team provided, it would not help your business if he or she shrugged and said, "They're okay." Although that reply means they were satisfied, their lack of enthusiasm is not exactly a convincing endorsement.

You want to WOW the people you serve. You want to exceed their expectations. And you want to make them feel important. You want to make a difference in people's lives. If you do not, they are likely to go elsewhere the next time they need the product or service you provide.

Three simple steps to take when interacting with a customer:

(1) Smile,

(2) Respect the customer, and

(3) Exceed their expectations.

By doing these three simple things, you can create customer loyalty. During the COVID-19 pandemic, many businesses had no choice but to close their doors. Some went out of business. Some were only closed on a temporary basis. During this time, the restaurants in my community were forces to close their doors to patrons who wanted to come in for a sit-down meal; however, they were able to still provide meals for take-out or delivery. One well-known restaurant thrived during this period, and it was no secret why. Everyone loved the owner. He was visible within the community, sponsored many events and programs, donated to local charities, and treated his employees and customers with care and respect. When it came time for the community to support him, they rallied and did just that.

> "If you aren't making a difference in other people's lives, you shouldn't be in business. It's that simple." —Richard Branson

In a small surf town of Seal Beach in Southern California, a community showed the same type of support for a local mom-and-pop donut shop that had been in business for twenty-eight years when the owner's wife became ill. They first offered to raise some money to help with medical bills, but the owner was a proud man and did not want to take a handout, so he and his wife turned down that generous offer. The community decided they would help another way. They decided to come to the shop every day and buy out his entire inventory. Customers began arriving as early as 4:30 AM to purchase donuts by the dozens to bring to their work, churches, and schools. As soon as the donuts sold out, the owner was able to close the shop for the day and head home to care for his wife. It was not unusual for the donuts to sell out before 7:00 AM. This heartwarming story is one of many where a community rallies to take care of one of their own. Stories like this often reinforce the point that what unites us as human beings is far greater than what divides us.

Servant leadership and the Decision-Making Process

It is time for you to focus on providing exceptional service. If you expect your team to go above and beyond and treat your customers with the utmost care and respect, then you must set the example and treat them – your team members – the same way. You must provide them with the training, support, and resources they will need to successfully provide the best service possible. It is time to stop telling people how to act and start showing them by your own person example. It is time for you to refocus on the reason why your organization exists, which is to solve problems and fulfill needs. It is time to serve.

The servant leadership philosophy is different from traditional leadership where the leader focuses on the growth of the organization rather than the people who make up the organization. Servant leaders put the needs of the team members first. They can do this by sharing power and responsibility in a way that helps people develop their talent, skills, and ability so they can perform at a higher level. Again, it cannot be stressed enough that this does not mean servant leaders do not hold their people accountable. It simply means that they emphasize the personal growth and well-being of their members and expect their members to follow suit by putting the needs of the people they serve ahead of their own.

This is how a servant leadership model and mindset would work in the fire service industry:

A great chief will ask, "How can I serve my officers?"

A great company officer will ask, "How can I serve my firefighters?"

A great firefighter will ask, "How can I serve the public?"

It is not unusual to come across a story where firefighters do more than anyone would have expected them to do. For example, firefighters from Baytown, Texas, responded to a 911 call to assist a man who'd suffered a heart attack while mowing his lawn. After taking him to the hospital, they returned to the man's home and finished mowing his lawn. This act of kindness went viral after a neighbor took a photo of the act and posted it online. Perhaps that incident inspired the group of firefighters from Greenfield, Wisconsin who also treated a man suffering from a heart attack and returned to his home after transporting him to the hospital to finish shoveling his driveway. When asked why they did it, the members talked about wanting to make it easier for the man's wife to be able to get her car in and out of the garage so she could visit and care for her husband as he recovered.

You do not have to search hard to find stories about public servants who went above and beyond to serve the members of their community. There are the firefighters from my town of Kearny, New Jersey, who organized a parade for an eleven-year-old girl who was battling a brain tumor, or the ones from Houston, Texas, who mentored and tutored a preteen who ended up being inducted into the National Honor Society, or those in Wichita, Kansas, who delivered free pizzas to people who had working smoke detectors during fire prevention week. Those stories and thousands or others are a continuous reminder that the lifeblood of an organization can be summed up with one simple word: CARE.

The men and women of the fire service are lucky to be in a business where they have many opportunities to do something that can add value to the lives of others. What most people in other professions do not realize is that they also have that ability. You do not have to wait for a crisis to happen in a person's life before you show up and help alleviate their concerns. You just need to listen, be aware, and look for ways to make a person's day better.

With a servant leadership mindset, it is easier for any organization to make better decisions for their customers. This begins by you setting the right priorities. The first question is, "Is this good for our community or customer?" if the answer is no, do not do it. If the answer is yes, go to question two, "Is this good for our organization?" If the answer is no, do not do it. If the answer is yes, move on to the next question. If you have a crew within the company, ask, "is it good for my team?" If the answer is no, do not do it. If the answer is yes, move on to the final question, which is, "Is this good for me?" If the answer is yes, you have a winning idea. If the answer is no, reconsider your options before making the final decision.

The decision-making process:

- Is it good for the Community/Customer?
- Is it good for the organization?
- Is it good for my team?
- Is it good for me?

One Christmas I gave my wife a gift card for a Spa. With three kids, and a busy schedule, it seemed like it was a perfect gift. However, the gift card was placed in a sock drawer and eventually made its way to the bottom of that draw, threatening to never be seen again. In time, neither of us even remembered she had it. Three years later she received a call from a receptionist at the spa, who called to remind her that she still had an unused gift card. When my wife said she does not even know where the card is, they told her not to worry, so she made an appointment. She was so impressed she shared the story on social media and four of her friends ended up joining her for a day at the spa. They had such a great time that they decided to make it a yearly tradition.

There are two things about that story that I would like you to think about. First, the fact that the spa did not need to make that call. They could have just kept the money without providing a service. No one would have known. However, by making one simple phone call they acquired five new regular customers. The second thing I would like you to consider is the fact that people are always looking to post an experience on social media – good or bad. When they interact with you or someone who represents your organization or community, they are going to share the event with their network. Everyone is looking for a status update, good or bad. Give them a good one. If there is a third lesson to be learned from the story, it would be that socks are not the only thing to go missing from a sock drawer.

Do not settle for satisfying a need. Anyone can do that. You want to exceeded expectations. In the book *The Go-Giver*, authors Bob Burg and John David Mann call this the Law of Value, which can be summed up with the sentence, "Your true worth is determined by how much more you give in value than you take in payment."

> "Your true worth is determined by how much more you give in value than you take in payment." —*The Go-Giver*

To further expand on this topic, here are four qualities that would benefit servant leaders.

1. Trustworthiness
2. Empathy
3. Decisiveness

4.   Innovative thinking

- Trustworthiness: Be honest, truthful, and committed to doing what is best for all parties involved. People need to know they can rely on you. It is essential to use trust as the building block for all your relationships. If your team members do not trust you, your team will be consumed with drama, which will then move them into the decay stage. If your customers do not trust you, your business will suffer and eventually fail. Trust is built through everyday actions. Do your team members know that you care about them? If they do not, it would be because your daily actions are not telling them that you care. When it comes to trust, remember that your actions speak as loud as your words. You cannot just talk about core values like honesty and integrity, you must live them. Your actions will display how you feel and will provide direction for how you want all of them to treat each other as well as the people you serve.

- Empathy: It is good to treat people the way you would like to be treated, but it is better to treat them the way they would like to be treated. Empathy is showing an ability to understand and share the feelings of another. Be aware of what is happening in the lives of the people around you. Do not assume that a team member or customer who is unprofessional or rude is always like that. They may be in the middle of a personal crisis or at the tail end of a difficult time in their life. Try to see things from their perspective. Empathy is not just something to consider during tough times. Practicing empathy should be an everyday practice for a servant leader. Whenever possible, have brief face-to-face meetings instead of sending emails. This will give you the opportunity to thank people for their hard work and ask them if there is anything you could do to help them achieve their goals. That simple gesture will also help build trust because you are reminding them that you all play for the same team.

- Decisiveness: Strong leadership matters, especially in times of uncertainty and change. There are two reasons why many people in influential often positions fail: they do without ever thinking, or they think without ever doing. When it is time to take action – GO! If you need to adapt, do it. Every organization needs leadership that is ready to act. We have already established that you do not need to have all the answers. You have a team of people and endless resources at your disposal that you can consult with or refer to if needed. Just remember that someone must be willing to lead your organization to a better place, and that someone is you. Do not wait for things to be perfect. They never will be. Always remember that procrastination is the slayer of confidence.

- Innovative thinking: All leadership requires creativity and forward thinking. Think outside the box and try to determine better ways to serve your team and customers. What can you do different than other organizations in the same field as you? More importantly, what can you do better? Talk to your team members about ways they feel they can provide better service. Are there more effective ways for them to perform their duties? Get feedback from the people in the trenches. Ask your customers how you can better serve them. Talk to other leaders in your industry who are willing to give you advice. Then take the best ideas and run with them. Build a culture where everyone feels comfortable bringing a new idea to the table and sharing opinions without malice, judgment, victimization, or condemnation. Do this, and everyone will win in the long run.

To become an organization that is known for providing exceptional service, encourage your team to ask themselves and each other this one simple question every time they are dealing with a customer: "How can we go above and beyond to prove to this customer that we truly care?"

If you have a servant heart, and act on it; you will rarely go wrong.

Unhappy Customers and Difficult People

No one likes to hear that they are not doing a good job, so you can imagine the feeling that the regional presidents and store managers at a large, nationwide moving equipment and storage rental company had in the pit of their stomach when they discovered that the panel of eight strangers sitting on the stage at their annual convention in Arizona were a group of unhappy customers who had written bad reviews about their experiences with the company.

As it turned out, the company had paid for their trip to Arizona so their employees could hear these reviews firsthand, straight out of the customers' mouths. The CEO wanted his team members to hear un-edited reviews so the employees could hear – and feel – what it was like to be in the customer's shoes. As one after another shared their experiences with the audience, the message became loud and clear... we can do better... we must do better.

One cannot help but to respect the leadership of a company that is focused on finding better ways to serve by fixing their relationship with unhappy customers. After all, unhappy customers are not the goal for any organization, but they are your greatest source for learning what you are doing wrong.

> **Unhappy customers are your greatest source for learning what you are doing wrong.**

Almost everything in leadership comes back to relationships. A wise business owner would echo that statement when it comes to customers. It all comes down to building strong relationships that LAST. It is always a challenge for an organization when a customer is unhappy and vocal about it. If an upset customer calls or storms into an office and begins passionately telling you what they are upset about, an employee may be tempted to put their guard up like the woman working in the lost baggage department; however, there is a better way to deal with unhappy customers and difficult people. It is a simple, four-step process that you and your team members can use to help resolve the issue and build relationships that LAST. The steps are: Listen, Apologize, Solve, and Thank.

LISTEN: The individual will want to be heard so let him or her vent. Do not forget the golden rule of customer service, which is: the customer is always right. The person who is expressing dissatisfaction feels the way they do for a reason. Hear that person out. You may discover that their reaction is 100 percent justifiable because of the way one of your team members previously interacted with them or because the service your organization provided was not acceptable.

APOLOGIZE: You and/or your team may be at fault, or you may not be. Either way, it never hurts to say to someone, "I'm sorry you had that experience," or "I'm sorry you feel that way." When you do that, you are showing empathy and making the person understand that they matter to you. You may discover that by doing that one simple thing, the customer's demeanor will already begin to change for the better. You have not resolved the problem yet, but you have acknowledged that the problem exists, and you are ready to move to the next step and take corrective action.

SOLVE: Do what you can to make things right. Almost every problem has a solution, and your job is to find one that you and the customer can mutually agree upon. Another simple question such as "What can I do to make this better?" may be all it takes to start this process. In my experience, the Walt Disney Company has set the standard on this. Although my family and I have had amazing experiences during our trips to Disney, we had one experience that could have potentially soured one vacation. We booked a room at one of their resort hotels and paid extra for a view of the water;

however, we arrived to discover that a massive tree just outside our window blocked our view of the water. I called the front desk and in less that fifteen minutes two employees came up with a new room key and took us and our bags to a new room with a breathtaking view. They went out of their way to ensure our trip got off to a great start, and it did.

THANK: After the problem is resolved, thank the person for bringing it to you in the first place. Unhappy customers are a great source for discovering flaws within your organization, which can lead to a valuable learning experience for all who are involved. It does not matter if you are in sales, manufacturing, or the fire service. When dealing with unhappy customers, your goal will be to make a friend, so they will continue being a supportive customer.

There are consequences for poor customer service, which include negative press on social media, loss of trust, a bad reputation, a decrease in morale, an increase in regret, and problems that did not exist before. With regards to public servants, bad press can also lead to political issues that can be devastating for a police or fire department. You will have bigger problems than you bargained for if the people who vote on your budget, agree to your pay, and/or approve the purchasing of new equipment suddenly turn against you.

Another problem that comes with unacceptable customer service is a potential *ripple effect*. One angry customer will tell everyone he or she talks to about their experience with you and your organization. One customer's dissatisfaction can spread out like a ripple on social media that can potentially travel farther than you could possibly imagine and appear impossible to stop. This was true before the internet existed, but social media has given every person the ability to reach the masses with minimal effort.

There are different types of unhappy customers. There are those who thrive on spreading the negative by sharing their unpleasant experience with everyone who comes within three feet of them. There are others who demand apologies, sometimes in a public or political forum. Then there are the ones who you will never make happy, no matter what you say or do. However, it is in your best interest to do everything in your power to turn a disgruntled customer into a fan of your organization and try to build a LAST-*ing* relationship.

I've Got Your Back

Listening to the community you serve is essential for the survival of your organization, and it all starts with taking care of those under your charge. Do your team members know that you have their backs? If not, that is the first thing you need to make clear. This does not mean they get a pass if they do something illegal, immoral, or unethical. You are not helping anybody if you coddle them. Having a person's back does not mean they are not held accountable for their actions. It is the complete opposite. When someone is not doing the right thing, a good teammate would make them aware of it so the issue can be resolved before it causes a serious problem.

Do not think for a second that others are not watching you. Your team members have a vantage point for viewing your behavior and weigh it against your commitments. If they see you dealing unethically with vendors, lying to customers or community members, cheating, or failing to keep your word, the best and most principled of them will leave. The rest, even worse, will stay behind and follow your lead. You should want to lead by example and strive for interlocking accountability throughout your organization.

"I've got your back" means you look out for each other. If you were to ask the starting players of an MLB baseball team what their purpose is, they might answer, "to win a pennant or the World Series." Although that may be the goal, the purpose should be something completely different. Their purpose, and yours, should be to build strong and meaningful relationships so that every player on the team is playing for the other members who take the field wearing the same uniform. This is especially true for the leader of the organization.

If your child became ill and you had to leave work for a couple of days to care for him or her, would it mean something to you if your boss called to ask if you or your family needed anything? Of course, it would.

When was the last time you asked your team members or support staff what they needed to help them complete a task or achieve a goal? When you do ask, do you also listen? Do they have the time, support, training, resources, and guidance they need to become successful? Show me an individual who works only for himself or herself, and I will show you short-lived success. Show me a company with self-serving practices, and I will show you a short-lived business. Show me a boss who puts his or her team members first, and I will show you a team that will go to great lengths to make that boss proud of them. In the end, it is all about people, and the relationships you develop.

Chapter Recap

combustible tips to ignite your team

Remember the saying – Service to many leads to greatness – as you navigate your way through life's challenges. A person is assigned to a leadership position for a reason, which is to serve the needs of those around them. Service is not something you say, it is something you do. Do not hide in your office and send out memos and notices. Get out there, meet with your team face-to-face. Listen to their ideas and concerns and ask them what you can do to help them succeed. Then go beyond that and ask them about themselves. What makes them excited. What types of things do they place high on their value list? What are they enthusiastic about?

Invest in your team members. The way you treat them will set the example for how you want them to treat each other. They need to know you care. The most valuable gift you can give others is your time and attention. The same can be said about the way you treat your customers. The lifeblood of your business can be summed up in the word CARE. You must care about the individual and their needs. You must care about the product or service you are providing. You must care about the reputation you have for exceeding expectations, which should be your primary goal. Always seek to exceed expectations, not sometimes, always.

Those who are in a leadership position have the responsibility to make a difference. When someone has the means to effectuate positive social change, they also have the responsibility to do so. If you still are not sold on the benefits of servant leadership, take a moment to contemplate the days when you will be looking back on your life. How do you want to be remembered? Hopefully, you want to be remembered as someone who made a positive impact in the lives of other people. To do that, you will have to practice compassion and empathy, while at the same time holding people to a high standard. Fancy titles or bars on your collar do not make you a leader. The quality of your leadership is determined by the amount of people you inspire, encourage, motivate, improve, and serve. If you disagree with that, maybe you are not leading, maybe you are simply a person with a fancy title or bars on your collar.

8

REWARD YOUR TEAM

The people who work the hardest are often
those who feel the most appreciated.

I once received a heart-breaking phone call from one of my clients in the medical care industry. He worked in the pediatric department of a busy hospital that I regularly provided training for. It began with a simple text that read, "Can you talk?"

I immediately replied "yes," and within seconds my phone rang.

The tone and rhythm of his voice were sure indications that he was feeling stressed. He began by referencing a story that I told during one of my seminars. It was a story about a close friend who had dealt with post-traumatic-stress-disorder.

"I just needed to talk with you about something that I have been going through this past week," he said.

He and I talked for the next twenty minutes or so. Correction, he talked. I listened. It cannot be stressed enough that one of the most under-used skills in society today is listening with the intent of understanding. Most people half-listen, as they wait for the pause so they can offer their rebuttal or add to the story the other person is telling them with one of their own. People in leadership positions need to do a better job of shutting their mouths and opening their ears and minds to what is being said.

The doctor went on to tell me that he had a tragic incident occur at work and he was having a difficult time dealing with it. The incident involved the loss of an infant and to be quite honest, I would not feel good about providing details about what occurred. What I will share is that he was dealing with stress, sleepless nights, flashbacks, avoidance, and negative thoughts – all symptoms of PTSD.

As we spoke, I asked if anyone at work was helping him though this. He told me that he did not want to burden his colleagues with his challenge. I asked him if any of his co-workers were struggling with the incident, and he said most of them were not working there when it happened. Prior to this statement, I thought it was a recent occurrence.

167

"When did it happen?" I asked.

"Seven years ago," he replied.

I was struck by two things: (1) He considered this a burden that he did not want to share with his co-workers; and (2) the incident occurred seven years ago but was just now manifesting in the form of PTSD.

Being a doctor or nurse, especially one who works in trauma center, is as stressful as any other high-stakes profession. You would be hard-pressed to find another profession where team members experience the most tragic occurrences in life than these men and women in the medical industry do. For that reason alone, I hope anyone in that industry would not feel that they would be a burden to their colleagues if they were having a difficult time coping with a traumatic incident. Medical professionals need to look out for each other. We all do.

In society, it is easy to wonder why we seem to only rally around each other when there is a tragic occurrence. For example, it should not take a terrorist attack for New York and Boston area sports fans to show respect for each other. We are all human beings trying to figure out this thing called life. We belong to the same species. We should be looking out for each other all the time, not just when things go wrong. Although human beings worldwide may never feel that they all belong to the same tribe, it is important that your team members do. If a traumatic event can resurface years after it occurred, I hope you are surrounded by people you can have an open and direct conversation with about how you are feeling, and I hope they have your back.

If you do not have that type of environment on your team right now, create it. It does not take much. Just the fact that I felt compelled to start this chapter with the story about my doctor friend was all I needed to remind me that I needed to reach out to him and say hello, which I did ten minutes before writing this paragraph (and again when I was re-reading this section two months later).

Perhaps the thought of a friend who has been dealing with a challenge of their own has come into your mind as you read the previous paragraphs. If so, I would like to encourage you to pause before you continue, call your friend, and check on his or her well-being. If you have team members in similar situations, do the same with them. Let them know you care. This book will still be here when you are done.

Pause here, make your call(s), and continue reading when you are ready.

Be the type of leader who puts other people's needs in the forefront. As mentioned in the previous chapter, fancy titles or bars on your collar do not make you a leader. The quality of your leadership is determined by the amount of people you inspire, encourage, motivate, improve, help, and serve.

Be the person who looks out for their team members and rewards them for a job well done. Show them that you appreciate their effort and attitude. One of the leading causes of low morale in the workplace is when people feel under-appreciated. On that note, common sense would lead one to believe that the people who work the hardest are often those who feel the most appreciated. Leaders who take care of their people have the advantage of creating a successful working environment.

There are three things that will make or break every organization and team. They are: 1. Strong Leadership,

　　　　　　　　2. Dedicated People, and

　　　　　　　　3. A Winning Culture

Numbers 1 and 2 will determine number 3.

> The quality of your leadership is determined by the amount of people you inspire, encourage, motivate, improve, help, and serve.

Why People Work

What motivates you to go to work or volunteer your time? There could easily be more than a thousand ways to answer that question; however, most of those answers will fall into one of these six categories:

- Time
- Money
- Security
- Recognition
- Belonging to a team
- Making a difference

You may ask, "How does someone work for time?" Imagine a man or woman who swaps work hours with another employee, or one who works eight hours of overtime so they could make a few extra dollars and go on a weekend getaway with their significant other. Perhaps they are putting in extra hours in exchange for comp time off. Those are three examples of trading time in one area in exchange for time in another area.

Everyone already understands what it means to work for money or security; however, three primary motivators for people who work or volunteer their time are recognition, belonging to a team, and making a difference.

> Three primary motivators for people who work or volunteer their time are recognition, belonging to a team, and making a difference.

It would benefit you to identify which of those six motivates you, as well as the other members of your team. The best and easiest way to do this is by asking them. One of the first things I did with each newly hired recruit who was assigned to my shift was sit down with that individual and get to know a little bit about who they were. During our conversation one of the questions that I would always ask is, "Why did you want to become a firefighter?"

This was not an interview question. They already had the job. In fact, before I even met most of these individuals, they had completed the academy, so the sole purpose of me asking them this question was simply for me to get to know a little about them as a person. I will never forget the time I asked this question to one of our newest team members only to hear the following response: "Honestly, Chief. I really need the security. I have young son and a fiancée. We would love to get married, buy a home, and expand our family, but to do that I needed something more stable than what I had. I honestly don't know if I will be any good at this, but it seems like a great job, and I wanted to give it a shot."

Truth be told, I was pleasantly surprised by his honesty. Partially because I understand that security is one of the six primary reasons why someone takes a job in the first place. He could easily have said that he really likes to help people – which most people in service-based industries do, but that would not have told me nearly as much about him as his actual answer did. His answer made me understand that we shared similar values. More specifically, we both wanted to provide for our families. I also knew that he was not afraid to take chances and try something new. When I asked him what made him think this seemed like a great job, he made reference to the fact that it quickly became apparent to him in the academy that this was a team-based profession where people need to work together and rely on each other in order to achieve success. This made me realize he was also a team player.

Knowing that this recruit was motivated by security gave me some insight as to why he was here, but the next step for me was essential. After getting to know a little about each recruit, I would talk with them about the expectations I, and our organization, had for each of them. During this part of the conversation, I would often show the recruit the performance evaluation that their officers would use to evaluate and measure their progress throughout the next twelve months. I would also talk to them about the importance of displaying certain characteristics and traits such as trust, reliability, and humility. Setting expectations is importation, but so is the next step, which is recognizing those who meet and/or exceed those expectations.

This recruit did just that.

Every day he came to work with a smile on his face and gave us 100 percent. He met and exceeded the expectations I set for him and as a result, the other team members and I would often praise him for his effort and make him aware that he brought value to our team. A few months after joining our team, he brought his fiancé and son to the fire station for a visit. After introducing me to his family, he brought his son over to the apparatus floor to show him the fire engine. During this time, I had the opportunity to talk one on one with his fiancé.

"We love having your fiancé on our team. He comes to work with a smile, trains with enthusiasm, and gives me 100 percent every day," I told her.

She replied by saying, "I can't get him to stop talking about how much he loves working here."

Think about that for a moment. He took the job for security but ended up getting so much more. He was receiving five of the six primary reasons listed above (money, security, recognition, belonging to a team, and making a difference). If we did not provide him with the recognition or make him feel like he belonged to a team, he would still come to work every day (after all, security was his primary motivator), but he would most likely be significantly less enthusiastic about being there. I am sure you would agree that you know people who are very unhappy with their current job, but they show up every day because they need money and security. Imagine how much their life and productivity would improve if they received some of those other rewards.

Instead of creating a workplace full of miserable people who robotically show up and unenthusiastically go through their mundane daily routines, focus on the things you can provide your team members, such as recognition and a sense of belonging to something bigger than themselves. By doing so, you have a better chance of developing a loyal, more committed team member. Any time a co-worker or teammate fully commit to the team, the strength of that team multiplies.

Inspiration Versus Intimidation

Which type of leader will you be?

Take a moment to review these ten simple math problems.

$$10+0= 10$$
$$10+1= 11$$
$$10+2 = 12$$
$$10+3 = 13$$
$$10+4 = 14$$
$$10+5 = 14$$
$$10+6 = 16$$
$$10+7 = 17$$
$$10+8 = 18$$
$$10+9 = 19$$

What do you see when you looked at these simple math problems and answers?

Most people will immediately point out that 10+5 does not equal 14, and they are exactly right. The majority will bring attention to the one answer that is wrong. The question becomes: "Have they also noticed that the other nine answers are correct?"

Every one of us has worked for, or will work for, people like that. This world is full of bosses who will point out every-single-thing that you do wrong, but never point out the nine things you do right. The key is to know that those individuals exist and be prepared to deal with them – and the goal is to not become like them.

Let me make one thing very clear. I am a flawed individual which would make me a flawed leader by default. I have made mistakes, adapted, and learned from them. The difference is that I am not "intentionally flawed." In other words, every human being on the planet is flawed. We all make mistakes. The ones who concern me are those who rise to a position of influence within their organization and choose to try to diminish and intimidate the people they are supposed to be inspiring and leading to a better place.

Do you know a person who would fall into that category? If so, you probably also know that you would hate (or do hate) working for that individual. Sadly, those types of people also seem to groom, or align themselves with, others who think likewise. When this happens, that organization begins to fall into the decay stage of team development and your team becomes consumed with drama.

A person with the opportunity to lead an organization has a choice to make. They can choose to lead by way of Inspiration or Intimidation.

- in-spi-ra-tion (noun) The process of being mentally stimulated to do or feel something, especially to do something creative.
- in-tim-i-da-tion (noun) The action of intimidating someone, or the state of being intimidated.

The thing about Intimidation is that is a tool that weak and insecure people use to try to stay in power. They feel that by maliciously and intentionally applying pressure, they can keep a separation between them and the people they are supposed to be leading. Some forms of workplace intimidation include verbal abuse, threats, physical violence, unrealistic deadlines, unjust criticism, sabotage of a person's work, sexual harassment, and holding some people to a much higher standard than others. Workplace intimidation causes employees and coworkers to feel inadequate and afraid and will ultimately erode the confidence of employees and affect their ability to do their jobs.

> Intimidation is a tool that weak and insecure people use to try to stay in power.

When you intimidate and punish your team members for making mistakes, you create a cautious, fearful, environment where those around you become less likely to make decisions and act upon them, because they fear the consequences that those actions might bring upon them. When this occurs, teams or individuals are no longer playing to win. Instead, they begin playing "not to lose." As a comparison, consider the prevent defense in football. The long-standing joke is that all teams do when they transition to a prevent defense is prevent their own team from winning.

Fear, greed, and ego are three reasons why a person might choose to intimidate their team members instead of leading them. Stronger leaders, on the other hand, will seek ways to inspire the people around them. Inspiration is a tool used by strong, confident people who put the needs of the team ahead of their own personal agenda. These people are secure enough to praise others and distribute credit to those who deserve it. Some of the tactics they use to inspire their team members are as follows:

1. Recognize people when they do a good job.

2. Celebrate team victories and create new traditions.

3. Find out what motivates people and tap into that individual's discretionary energy.

4. See and share the big picture (remind people WHY they are doing things).

5. Promote personal growth and motivation.

6. Set small, attainable, measurable goals.

7. Work hard but take breaks.

8. Stay positive.

9. Provide a sense of security.

10. Promote transparency and clarity.

11. Loosen the reins (do not micro-manage).

12. Have fun and create an environment where others can do the same.

The common internal question that most people in new leadership positions often ask themselves is, "How should I lead this team?" The answer to that question is actually quite simple. You should become the type of leader that you always wanted to work for.

Do not make the mistake that so many people make by thinking that you need to have all the answers. You do not, and you probably will not. If you are lucky, you will be leading a team of people who all have their own set of unique talent, skills, and abilities. Embrace the fact that some people on your team will be strong in areas where you are not, and vice versa. Do not ever forget that the best strategy is to put the right people in the right positions and get out of their way. You can do this by finding every team member's unique skill set and utilize their strengths in a way that the entire team benefits.

Insecure people who found their way into leadership positions are often threatened by talented people. They sometimes try to beat down the enthusiasm of the person who they fear will outshine them. As a result, the people who could have been the team's greatest assets become disengaged. As mentioned earlier in this book, the worst sound a leader can ever hear is silence coming from those who were once your most dedicated and passionate team members. That is the sound I have heard in some organizations that are being led by individuals who make decisions that benefit their personal agenda and ego more than it benefits the community they serve.

> Stronger leaders will seek ways to inspire the people around them.

It is a well-known fact that leading up the chain of command is significantly more challenging than leading down the chain of command. When you are the highest-ranking officer in the room, people have no choice other than to listen to you. If you happen to work for a person who leads through intimidation, please know that your value does not decrease based on someone's inability to see or acknowledge your worth. Their opinion of you does not have to become your reality. You can take the actions outlined in this book and begin to create your own reality.

Hopefully, you are actively seeking ways to become a better version of yourself. If your intent is to become an effective leader, work on your ability to develop trust and strong relationships with your team members. You want people to follow you not because they have to, but because they want to. My hope for you is that you work to enhance your ability to inspire those around you. Once again, if you ever lose sight of what type of leader you should be, remind yourself to be the type of leader you always wanted to work for. That thought should be enough to get you back on track.

Praise and Recognition

If you are a parent who has watched your child take his or her first steps, I am sure you were enthusiastically praising and celebrating that accomplishment. Rightfully so, because research has shown that a typical baby may attempt to walk somewhere between six hundred and nine hundred times before he or she is successful. You praise and recognize the accomplishment not only because it is a milestone in that child's life, but also because you have watched your child fail over and over before those steps were taken.

Now, take into consideration the level of determination that is needed for a grown man or women to fail between six hundred and nine hundred times without losing enthusiasm. Too many people give up after stumbling a few times and begin to tell themselves things like, "I can't do it," or "I give up." Too many people quit long before putting their fair share of consistent effort into trying to accomplish a specific task or learning a new skill. Take that into consideration when someone on your team persists and reaches a goal of theirs. It only makes sense to celebrate that achievement with them. It would be advisable for their boss, coach, manager, teammate, and/or leader to compliment that individual for a job well done.

Even the most selfless people appreciate being recognized for a job well done. After all, remember that recognition is a primary motivator for human beings. If you fail to recognize your team members for a job well done, you are missing the opportunity to show your appreciation and reinforce the correct behavior. There are many ways to show appreciation. Some organizations provide monetary rewards in the form of bonuses or raises. You may not have the ability or budget to do so, but you do have the ability to acknowledge them for their effort.

Many leadership development experts believe firmly in praising people for outstanding effort and performance; however, they would also warn against overpraising. It does not take a genius to figure out when and where to recognize outstanding effort, it comes down to being aware and paying attention. An experienced youth athletic coach would be able to determine which of their players have been excessively complimented and overpraised by their parents for every single thing they have ever done. Those kids could benefit from tough, honest, direct coaching. The same coach may also be aware of the kids who craved a compliment because they have never received one. Coaches should take time to learn about their players, and so should you. Find out why each individual team member decided to become a part of your team. Were they looking for time, money, or security? Do they crave recognition, want to belong to a team, or feel like they are making a difference?

Some of the people around you may have been pampered their entire life, or perhaps it is the opposite, and they are just craving an encouraging word. Whether they need tough love or a pat on the back, both will need your help. Praise is an effective tool to help keep your team motivated and on the right track. Rewarding your team for a job well done does not mean that you need to lower your standards and accept mediocrity. Rewarding high performing team members can help keep them motivated, but few things will demotivate great performers as much as a leader who tolerates poor performers.

In his book Carved in Stone: The 12 Virtues of West Point That Build Leaders and Produce Success, author Pat Williams wrote that the late UCLA head basketball coach John Wooden won ten NCAA national championships (including seven consecutive) and never swore at or demeaned his players. Wooden was famed and beloved for his compassionate coaching style.

Williams went on to point out that it is certainly possible to motivate people with fear, but love is a vastly more powerful motivator. When people feel safe around you, when they know they can take risks (and occasionally fail) and are not afraid you will demote them, humiliate them, or destroy them in front of their peers, you will develop a bond built on a foundation of trust and respect. Love, trust, and loyalty encourage people to use their ingenuity and creativity to accomplish great things. Fear causes people to hide their mistakes and try to play it safe.

It benefits no one to sugar coat such an important point, so here is the simple reality. If you do not provide some form of respect and recognition for your hard-working team members, they will eventually leave and go work for someone who does. This is as true in the fire service as it is in corporate America. There are plenty of firefighters who have transferred to other departments knowing they were going to make less money because they felt they were going to be treated with more respect.

Praising and recognizing people for a job well done is most effective when it occurs in front of others. This can happen in formal and informal settings. Formal recognition occurs in ceremonies, events, and staff meetings. Informal recognition is usually immediate, on the spot, in public and in front of others. When individuals and teams do something that was worthwhile, a strong leader will make a big deal out of it. Celebrate the successes and achievements of your colleagues. Put effort into recognizing others. Recognition is vital but to be effective it must be positive, sincere, and timely.

> ## Celebrate the successes and achievements of your colleagues.

Recognition is a powerful thing. Babies will cry for it and grown men and women have died for it. Certainly, we do not want anyone to ever have to die for recognition, but wouldn't it be a shame if they died without ever having received any?

There is only one caveat to praise and recognition. If you provide it unequally or undeservingly, it can have an adverse reaction. Recognition is essential, but it must be warranted. That being understood, get excited about giving credit to those who deserve it. Be on the lookout for those who are putting forth an exception effort and achieving great things, and when you witness or hear about them, acknowledge them. They will appreciate you for it and everyone can win in the end.

Recognize Outstanding Effort
The Finest Officer

I was providing leadership training for the members of the Seattle Fire Department when Captain Mike Gagliano approached me during a break. Captain Gagliano was a senior member of the department and a well-respected culture creator in the United States fire service. He was known for having contagious enthusiasm for the job and a passion for helping to develop a positive culture and strong leaders. Mike was one of those individuals who makes people feel good about themselves, which is why I was happy to see him walking in my direction with his trademark smile.

"Chief, can you do me a favor?" Mike asked.

"Anything buddy," I replied.

"I'd like to purchase one of your books for my newest lieutenant, but I would like you to sign it and present it to him as a gift."

"Okay, I can do that." It was a simple request.

"But," he continued, "I would like to you do it in front of everyone and say it is a gift for him because he is one of the finest officers the Seattle Fire Department has ever had."

Hmmmmm. That's a tricky one, I thought. There were approximately two hundred people in the room. If just a few of them disagreed with that assessment of this young officer, the gesture could backfire with disastrous consequences. Firefighters are some of the most selfless people I have ever known, but they are also brutally honest. It comes with the territory. They do not just watch tragedy happen on television. They live through it. They are the ones who serpentine down a busy highway at high speeds when they hear that a child has been struck by a vehicle. They are the ones who pull the lifeless bodies out of the charcoal-black smoke-filled homes, rip off their masks and try to revive them in front of fifty curious neighbors and onlookers. They see and experience enough of life's harsh realities that, over time, their tolerance for bull-crap ceases to exist. Some become calloused, others become salty, but either way, a worldly firefighter is likely to call your bluff when warranted.

Mike continued to try to sell me on his request. "He has been working very hard, doing really great things and he deserves to be recognized for his effort and commitment," he said.

I did not personally know this officer, but I did know Captain Gagliano. I respected him and I trusted his judgment, so I agreed to acknowledge and recognize the young lieutenant in front of his peers. After the break, all the firefighters returned to their seats. I spoke for a few minutes about the difference between positional leaders and inspirational leaders before asking if this lieutenant was in the room.

A gentleman near the middle of the room raised his hand.

"Can you please stand for a moment?" I asked.

He curiously lifted his body from the seat. I held up a copy of Step Up and Lead and said, "This book is a gift for you because I have been told that you are one of the finest officers the Seattle Fire Department has ever had."

His eyes widened. He did not expect the compliment. In fact, it blew him away. What happened next, however, blew me away. Everyone began to clap in acknowledgment of this young officer. It was slow at first, but it grew into a standing ovation. Everyone turned to face him and showed their appreciation for the example he had been setting.

The response by everyone in the room made me realize that this lieutenant either truly is a fine officer, or Seattle firefighters are the nicest people in the world. Although I absolutely did find this group of firefighters to be incredibly welcoming, it was obvious that they all respected the young lieutenant and agreed that he deserved this unscripted, unexpected display of appreciation.

Later that evening, I was thinking about what had happened and three thoughts came to mind. The first was how much I respected Captain Gagliano for the way he wanted to provide one of the members on his team with that moment without anyone knowing he was the man behind it. He understood the value of second-hand praise as well as the power of giving credit to those who deserve it. I also thought about what that moment did for this lieutenant. Perhaps it was a moment of validation which provided him with a much needed second wind. After all, doing the right thing is not always the easy thing. The third thought I had was about all the other people in the room. I wondered what that moment did for all of them. I am certain there were others in attendance that day who would love to have a moment like that – one where they are recognized as a good example of how to do their job by their peers. After all, who would not want a moment like that? Perhaps some of them left the class that day determined to become a better version of themselves by emulating some of the traits and characteristics that this young officer was just recognized for.

Moments like that remind me of one of my favorite quotes – a candle loses nothing by lighting another candle. Have you ever wondered why some people find it difficult to take the spotlight off themselves and place it on another person? Could it be fear of becoming expendable? Perhaps it is an overinflated ego that needs to be constantly fed. Whatever the reason, it would benefit you to recognize that nobody enjoys working hard for a leader, or playing for a coach, who does not show appreciation to their team members.

> "A candle loses nothing by lighting another candle." —James Keller

Do Not Reward Poor Performers

On the surface this may seem obvious. If a person is not performing up to acceptable standards, it must be addressed. A common cause for low morale in the workplace is when the people who complain the most and do the least are rewarded with less work and less responsibility. Do not make the mistake of rewarding people who do not do their job.

Imagine you work in law enforcement and one of the officers on your group is lazy, does not train enough, and fails to adhere to department policies. He regularly shows up late for work with bags under his eyes, wearing a wrinkles uniform and sporting a five-o'clock shadow. His supervisor has been on him for weeks. The officer talks a good game, but never changes his behavior. Another officer takes a photo of him sleeping at his desk at 10:00 AM. The photo gets passed from member to member until everyone sees it. Your department has three stations spread out throughout the community, and he works out of the busiest one, which means the others have no choice but to pick up the slack for his dismal lack of effort.

Now imagine the chief of the department calling the officer and his supervisor into his office. He tells the officer that he is making some moves and is reassigning the officer to another station, which also happens to be the slowest station. As a reason for the move the chief says, "We have a lot of tactical equipment that has been neglected at that station and you are very good with that stuff, so the main reason I am transferring you to that station if because I need you to help get everything in order." The officer, feeling great about the compliment he just received, leaves happy, almost feeling as if he'd just received a promotion, without any inclination that he was doing anything wrong at all.

After the officer leaves the room, the supervisor is confused because he has been trying to correct this officer's behavior for a while, and now feels like all the chief did was move the problem from one station to another. The chief turns to the supervisor and says, "There's his second chance. His first order should be to tell his guys not to take photos of him when he's sleeping at work."

There is an example of poor leadership. Instead of addressing the problem, the chief made the individual feel as if he was being rewarded for his actions. Additionally, this type of action can shut down good employees who have been giving their best effort but now see that it does not pay off.

The wife of a friend of mine who works as a paralegal told me about the time that she complained to her bosses about a co-worker who was always on social media while she was working twice as hard to pick up the slack. The attorneys brought the slacking employee in for a discussion, ended up re-assigning her, and even gave her a few dollars more per week, making her feel as if she'd received a promotion. A week later, my friend's wife was given a rather difficult assignment to complete. They told her she was getting the assignment because they needed it done right and the other employee is not as reliable as she is.

The slacker received a pay raise while the reliable employee received more work. How do you think that made the reliable employee feel? She told me that the other employees would talk in the break room about how they should all do less work and spend more time on social media like the slacking employee so they could receive promotions as well.

Rewarding your team does not mean rewarding lazy, poor performers who do not step up to do what they are supposed to do. Doing so will cause your reliable team members to shut down. If you have a problem employee, you need to address the issues that pertain to him or her as soon as possible.

Take corrective actions that will result in a positive change in behavior.

Treat People Right

Profit, pleasing stakeholders, productivity, and output are important, but success ultimately depends on the effort put forth by those who do the work. When an organization places their value on the bottom line more than its people, it is only a matter of time before their best people go elsewhere, leaving behind those who are apathetic or under-performers. This can cause a decrease in morale and increase in disciplinary issues, which may cause some of your better people to leave.

Fear of loss is a powerful thing. If you own a business and have one or two outstanding employees, you may have lost sleep fearing that you could lose them to a competitor. The same can be said for the coaching staff of a successful team with regards to their star player. The first thing you need to acknowledge is that no one is irreplaceable. Your starting players today will most likely not be your starting players ten years from now; however, this reality does not change the fact that no team wants to lose their most valuable team members.

It has been well documented that a high percentage of people who have left their company on their own merit have done so because of poor leadership/management. This creates many problems for the company. One being cost. There is a price associated with training new employees. The interesting thing is that many people who leave, do not necessarily leave because they found a job that offered better pay or benefits. Many times, they leave and go work somewhere else for less money simply because they did not feel appreciated.

Retention is one of the keys to developing a successful team. Volunteer organizations may struggle with this because they provide little to no financial compensation for their people; however, people do not generally volunteer their time with the thought of financial compensation at the forefront of their mind. So, how can the leader of volunteer organizations improve their retention rate? It begins by contemplating why people volunteered in the first place. For starters, remember the six motivators we covered earlier – Time, Money, Security, Recognition, Belonging to a Team, and Making a Difference. One of the single most important influences for job satisfaction and retention is purpose. A person who feels they belong to a team and is making a difference has purpose. Employees who derive meaning and significance from their work are more likely to stay with their organizations.

If you are the owner and CEO of your own company, chances are you have purpose, but do you radiate it? If not, put yourself in the shoes of the person on your team who is working long hours and is on the lower end of the pay scale. What are you doing to connect them with that purpose? Do you include them? Do you ask for their opinion on important issues and listen to what they have to say? Do you ever stop to think that they may have an idea that can help you achieve the goal you are striving to reach?

> # Employees who derive meaning and significance from their work are more likely to stay with their organizations.

Building trust should be your top priority. Without trust, nothing else matters. You cannot wait until your top achievers decide to leave before you cultivate trust. At that point in the game, it is too late. You should start doing so before they are even officially on your team. Trust is a key ingredient in developing a winning culture. When you have a great culture, you will also have a low turnover rate.

There are basically only two reasons why someone would voluntarily leave your team:

1. They feel it is time for a change, or
2. Something is wrong.

If you have strong trustful relationships, people would be more inclined to talk with you about their concerns prior to making the decision to move in another direction. Even before that, during your day-to-day interaction, you would probably see early warning signs and be able to determine if there is something wrong. Early detection of problems would provide you with the opportunity to address small issues before they become large ones. When people trust each other, they talk; and dialog, discussion, and debate are how teams solve real problems.

Trust negates the need for excess policies, thereby allowing you to soften your stance on unnecessary discipline. Although discipline is not a dirty word, there is an absolute right way and wrong way to use it. It can be used as a precursor for good behavior, or a fear tactic by an insecure boss. Some people associate discipline with punishment because they worked for an individual who may have used it that way; however, for those who use discipline the correct way, punishment will not be necessary.

It all comes back to trust. You may be a high-ranking officer with management responsibilities, and you may be competent, but you must also be able to create an environment where everyone treats each other as equals. Imagine a team that is so strong nobody on the outside can determine who the leader is. That is a goal worth striving for, and it all starts with treating people right.

How important are your people to you? Are you approachable? After more than twenty-six years in the fire service, I believe in the chain of command and value the structure that it provides; however, I have also come to appreciate the importance of being approachable and keeping an open-door policy. In his book Up the Organization, author Robert Townsend states that each level of management lowers communication effectiveness within your organization by 25 percent.

Some high-level executives could use an ego check. They need to show some humility. Humility is powerful. This does not mean thinking less of yourself. It means thinking of yourself less. A smart executive will understand their position is important, but they will also understand that they alone do not make a winning team. The smartest chief officers I know have come to the realization that chiefs do not extinguish fires. firefighters on hose lines extinguish fires. Value your people. They are your greatest assets. Show respect to all the members of your team, from the star players to those who clean the office after everyone goes home.

Give your people permission to act, make decisions, grow, and improve. Do not restrict their creative freedom. Give them permission to try new things. If they are afraid of the consequences that accompany failure, they will not want to try to find new and better ways to do things because the risk will outweigh the rewards. If your team members make mistakes, support them. If they continue to make the same mistake, you can deal with that based on the Unaware, Unable, Unwilling concept mentioned earlier in this book, but permission to act is a powerful blessing from a team leader.

> Value your people.
> They are your greatest assets.

When a team member contributes ideas or performs w ell, do you acknowledge their effort, praise them in public, and give credit where credit is due? Are you providing them with guidance and helping them achieve their career aspirations? Do you talk with them about things that are important to them? Do you remind them that they play an essential role on your team – even those who are currently sitting on the bench? If they are your rock stars, are you encouraging them to help you build bench strength?

If you are not doing these things, now is the time to start doing them.

Celebrate Your Victories

It is a great feeling when a team achieves a goal. Even the casual sports fans can appreciate the celebration that occurs when teams win championships. Those teams are celebrating the preparation, time, effort, blood, sweat and sacrifice that led to the realization of that moment.

Everyone deserves to feel the thrill of victory, but just because you have a lead does not mean you have already won the game. When you become a fully developed team, the last thing you want to do is become complacent or fall into a false sense of security by thinking that you can stop preparing because you won a big game. As Babe Routh once said, "Yesterday's home runs don't win today's games."

> "Yesterday's home runs don't win today's games." —Babe Ruth

Celebrating victories is one of the great rewards you can provide for a team. Your hardworking team members deserve a moment to be recognized and appreciated for their effort. Some victories may be grand in scale, other may seem like they were no big deal, but a victory is a victory and should be treated as so.

One of the great traditions of the fire service is that we believe in honoring our people while they are still with us. We do this through events like promotional celebrations, award ceremonies, and retirement parties. One of my friends who serves in a large department told me they had more than one thousand firefighters showed up to say goodbye to a firefighter who had to leave the job due to illness. It is not uncommon to have that many people show up to a funeral, but to show up for a person's last day at work says a lot about how firefighters treat their own.

Does your organization treat people that way? Commitment, hard work and perseverance should be rewarded, and victories should be celebrated. How you do that is your choice. You may choose to recognize people for their efforts during a weekly meeting, or an annual award ceremony. I once spoke for a team of managers for ExxonMobil and after our two-hour training session, they all jumped on a bus and attend a baseball game together. It was the plant managers way of showing appreciation for their hard work and effort throughout the previous twelve months.

After one challenging structure fire, I sent a text message to my crew with the following message: I just wanted to let you all know how proud I am of all of you. Your performance today was exceptional. Thank you for the exceptional daily effort you give me, our organization, the community we serve, and each other. Your attitude and dedication do not go unnoticed.

That text kicked off a group chat that consisted of encouraging words and praise they all had for each other. The comments were amazing. How you choose to celebrate your victories and provide recognition for people is up to you. The important thing is that you do it and do not take your hard-working team members for granted.

First Family First

In the fire service, we often refer to the coworkers on our shift as our second family, and rightfully so. Career firefighters can regularly spend forty-eight straight hours together. They eat three meals a day together, attend in-house classes together, train in the field together, clean the station together, and put their lives on the line together. Many of the men and women who work together also attend events outside of work together, whether it be work-related seminars, sporting events, or social events like weddings, graduations, or other celebrations. That is as close to becoming a family as you can get.

To become a second family, you must understand what a family consists of. In the context of human society, the purpose of families is to maintain the well-being of its members. Families provide the means to meet basic needs of its members. It provides boundaries for performing tasks in a safe environment. Family is also about relationships. A strong family foundation will consist of love, trust, commitment and understanding. When one family member falls, the rest are there to pick him or her up. When one succeeds, the others are there to celebrate. If you are lucky enough to develop that type of environment at home and at work, you are truly blessed.

The key is to remember that you are a second family. Point being: do not neglect your first family. When you achieve success at work, your first family will have made sacrifices. A coach does not win a championship without taking time away from his or her family. The same can be said about an entrepreneur. When I write books, I often lock myself in my office from dawn to dusk every day for several months until I have a finished product. My family makes sacrifices when I take time away from them, and so does yours. When you achieve a personal or career goal, reward your team at work, but make sure you reward your home team as well.

One bit of advice on celebrating your person victories. Take a page from the Detroit Lions running back Barry Sanders book. Sanders set the standard in the way he celebrated his victories. Every time the legendry NFL running back scored one of his 99 touchdowns, he jogged up to the referee and flipped him the ball. It was a symbolic gesture that displayed the humble, yet confident attitude of, "I've been here before, and I'll be here again."

You may not have scored touchdowns in the NFL, but you have had victories and defeats like everyone else. Celebrate your achievements and be proud of your past, no matter how difficult it may have been. Your past has given you the strength and wisdom you have today.

Chapter Recap

combustible tips to ignite your team

Every leader wants a team full of people who are willing to go the extra mile, but every leader does not take the time to cultivate that culture by showing appreciation for those who have already gone the extra mile. Sometimes, the extra mile begins with a simple compliment. Although people work for time, money, and security, there are three additional reasons why people work or volunteer their time. Those reasons are recognition, belonging to a team, and making a difference. People who are well compensated may still be tempted to look for work elsewhere if they do not feel appreciated for their efforts in their current job.

Some people in leadership positions use disciplinary tactics to motivate their team, but there is a difference between disciplining to punish, and disciplining to correct behavior. Progressive discipline, for example, is a step-by-step process designed to modify unacceptable employee behaviors. When used correctly, progressive discipline can he highly effective. Discipline as a form of strict punishment without the intent of correcting an individual's behavior; however, is not the best motivator. It is a scare tactic that will likely cause team members to do less because they fear repercussion. This type of culture commonly pushes people to the point where they longer care, and when your team members don't care, you don't have a team. You have a bunch of people who just show up.

We live in a society where everyone wants the rewards, but few seem to want to take responsibility and do the work that produces those rewards. When your team members take ownership and do more than expected; you should praise and encourage them, and you should do so in public. As a result, you will likely continue to get the same type of effort from them, and you may find that others who want to feel appreciated for their contributions will step up their game as well.

A worthy task for a team leader would be to find ways to show your appreciation for your hard-working team members and continue to find ways to motivate them to be the best they can be. If you do so, you will become amazed by what you can accomplish simply by providing credit to those who deserve it. It will serve you well to continuously remind yourself that the people who work the hardest are often those who feel the most appreciated.

CONCLUSION

The ball is in your court now.

You are familiar with the stages of team development, and you are aware of the eight essential steps that must be taken to achieve and sustain excellence. Becoming a high-performance team will not happen by accident. It requires specific, deliberate action steps. So, this is your call-to-action.

Whichever stage your team is in – incipient stage, growth stage, fully developed stage, or decay stage – the steps outlined in this book will help you lead them to victory. The wonderful thing about these steps is that even if you were tackling a solo project, you can follow the same advice in this book to help you achieve personal success.

Do not allow complacency to set in. High-performance teams will never stay in the fully developed stage unless they continue to apply the principles that enabled them to reach and sustain that level of success in the first place. Individuals and teams are either progressing or regressing. They are moving in the right direction, or the wrong direction, and that direction is determined by their daily habits.

The only stage you will want to avoid is the decay stage. No one wants to be there, but many teams may find that they are moving toward that direction from time to time. When this happens, it is essential that you and the others on your team do something about it, and now you know what to do. My hope is that you revisit this book, review the steps as needed, and take corrective action.

You and your team may be one degree away from reaching your Flash Point, so post these eight steps somewhere where you can see them daily. Let them be a simple reminder for you to set expectations, prepare for victory, take action, delegate to develop, have the guts to persist, adapt when necessary, serve all and serve well, and reward your team. By doing so, you can find your flash point, ignite a fire, and forge a winning team culture.

FLASH POINT

Ignite Your Team and Forge a Winning Culture

– STEP 1 –
SET EXPECTATIONS UP FRONT

Every organization's culture is created by design or default.

– STEP 2 –
PREPARE FOR VICTORY

Teams often win or lose long before their games begin.

– STEP 3 –
TAKE ACTION

Procrastination is the slayer of confidence.

– STEP 4 –
DELEGATE TO DEVELOP

Dividing tasks and developing people multiplies your chances of success.

– STEP 5 –
HAVE THE GUTS TO PERSIST

At some point in a fight, technique gives way to heart and determination.

– STEP 6 –
ADAPT WHEN NECESSARY

You must have a contingency plan for adversity because you will encounter some.

– STEP 7 –
SERVE ALL AND SERVE WELL

Always strive to exceed customer expectations–not sometimes, always.

– STEP 8 –
REWARD YOUR TEAM

The people who work the hardest are often those who feel the most appreciated.

Books by Frank Viscuso

- **Step Up and Lead** (Amazon Best-seller) Considered a "must read" by many of today's top fire service professionals, Step Up and Lead will introduce you to the top traits and necessary skills needed to lead in today's world. Learn how to properly critique others, build morale, handle insubordination, earn trust, prevent freelancing, tackle difficult administrative tasks, lead an organization through change, and much more. This popular book has been referred to as *the backbone of the fire service.*

- **Step Up Your Teamwork** (Amazon Best-seller) Through powerful stories and proven principles, Step Up Your Teamwork teaches readers how to create momentum, prepare for success, prevent team collapse, and turn a group of individuals into a high-functioning, productive team.

- **Common Valor: True Stories from America's Bravest (Volume 1)** (Amazon Best-seller) A powerful book that captures the human emotion and drama from firefighters who have endured a wide range of firefighting and rescue scenarios. This book goes way beyond the stories that the public may hear about. With Common Valor, you will feel as if you are right there, up close with the rescuers. From seeing brother firefighters die to being caught in a flashover and living to talk about it, Common Valor captures the true spirit and camaraderie of firefighters.

- **Fireground Operational Guides** (Amazon Best-seller) This book features 70 operational guides and a universal tactical worksheet that can be used in the field, to draft SOG's, and to prepare for promotional exams. The book comes with a CD that allows the reader to print out all the guides for use in the field and as study guides.

- **Practice Scenarios** (Amazon Best-seller) Practice Scenarios was written to help prepare firefighters handle problems in four major areas: fire incidents (structure fires, outdoor fires, vehicle fires), non-fire incidents (hazardous materials, collapse, vehicle accidents, compounded incidents), supervision scenarios, and administrative scenarios. This book will help the reader overcome challenges in the field and the assessment center.

- **It's Time to Step Up!** By popular request, Step Up and Lead has been adapted for leaders in "ALL" industries so they can learn and apply the same principles used in the fire service to everyday leadership. Strategy and tactics are not only needed when fighting a five-alarm structure fire. Sound strategy and tactics are also needed when motivating people, building morale, critiquing underperforming team members, mentoring new ones, delegating tasks, and making consistent progress as a team. It does not matter if you are a business owner, manager, sales team leader, public servant, or youth athletic coach –If your goal is to get your team to operate at the highest possible level, this book will help you achieve that goal.

- **The Mentor** (fiction) An inspirational story about a young couple that is struggling to make ends meet. After a chance encounter with a wealthy entrepreneur, Michael and Kristen Harper embark on a life changing journey.

- **Sprinkles the Fire Dog** (A children's book series written by Frank Viscuso and illustrated by Paul Combs) Sprinkles is a little puppy from a big city who dreams of one day becoming a fire dog. To achieve that dream, he must overcome his physical limitations, the critical corner mutts, and his own self-doubt. This is a wonderful and inspirational story about setting goals, putting in the work, and turning dreams into reality.

All books are available in print and digital formats. Step Up and lead, Step Up Your Teamwork, Common Valor, and The Mentor are also available in audio format.

For books and public speaking information and inquiries, visit www.frankviscuso.com or send an email to frank@commonvalor.com